football
oddities

football
oddities

Tony Matthews

The History Press

First published in 2005 by Tempus Publishing

Reprinted in 2009 by
The History Press
The Mill, Brimscombe Port,
Stroud, Gloucestershire, GL5 2QG
www.thehistorypress.co.uk

Reprinted 2010, 2011, 2012, 2013

All illustrations are by cartoonist Warren Gwynne © 'WAYNE', 2005.

British Library Cataloguing in Publication Data.
A catalogue record for this book is available from the British Library.

ISBN 978 0 7524 3401 8

Typesetting and origination by
Tempus Publishing Limited
Printed in Great Britain

Contents

Acknowledgements

I would like to thank Warren Gwynne ('Wayne') from Rowley Regis near Dudley in the West Midlands for his drawings and caricatures featured in this book.

Also I say thank you to everyone at Tempus Publishing, especially to Holly Bennion, Rob Sharman, Anthony Lovell and Katie Beard; to David Prole and Jack Rollin who have both compiled football oddity books in the past; and to my wife Margaret who has once again put up without me for hours on end as I've tip-tapped away at the computer keyboard and fingered through page after page of soccer books, magazines and programmes searching for these odd curios, facts and interesting snippets of the great game.

This book is dedicated to all those right-minded people who enjoy their football.

Introduction

A collection of oddities, coincidences, unusual occurrences, stranger-than-fiction stories and facts and figures ...all relating to the great game of Association Football.

The odd things that happen in football make the game a never-ending source of fascination. Novel twists affecting play and players continue to arise and each and every season literally hundreds of curios, odd facts, outrageous statistics and snippets of amazing, unbelievable and sometimes mind-boggling information crop up somewhere along the line.

Over the years a handful of books, brochures, magazines and supplements have been produced listing hundreds of so-called soccer odd-balls, numerous facts and figures, anecdotes and soccer curios. I have now placed many of them into one very interesting publication that will certainly get you talking...

Abandoned & Postponed Matches

The third round FA Cup tie between Newcastle United and Swansea Town at St James' Park in January 1953 was abandoned after just eight minutes through fog. A crowd of 63,499 had assembled to see the contest.

The Sheffield United v. West Bromwich Albion League game at Bramall Lane in March 2002 was abandoned after eighty-two minutes because the home side had been reduced to just six players (three had been sent off and two taken off injured). Albion were 3-0 ahead at the time and the result was allowed to stand.

The (Sheffield) Wednesday v. Aston Villa League First Division game on 26 November 1898 was abandoned with a little over ten minutes left with the home side 3-1 ahead. The authorities asked both clubs to play out the remaining time on 13 March 1899 when Wednesday added another goal to run out 4-1 winners.

A similar thing happened in Spain's La Liga in December 2004 when the Real Madrid v. Real Sociedad game was abandoned after eighty-three minutes with the scores level at 1-1. The remaining seven minutes were played later.

The Middlesbrough v. Oldham Athletic League game of 3 April 1915 was abandoned after fifty-five minutes when full-back Billy Cook of Oldham refused to leave the field after being sent off. The result was allowed to stand as Boro were leading 4-1 at the time. Cook was suspended for twelve months.

The 1979 Scottish Cup tie between Inverness Thistle and Falkirk was postponed no fewer than twenty-nine times before it was eventually played.

The third round of the FA Cup in 1963, scheduled for 5 January, was so severely hit by the atrocious weather conditions (snow, ice, frost) that the thirty-second and last tie was not completed until 11 March. The ties covered twenty-two dates, there were 261 postponements and one of them (Birmingham City v. Bury) was put off

no fewer than fourteen times – when it was finally staged the game was abandoned and eventually went to a replay.

The League game between Darwen and Leicester Fosse in January 1895 was abandoned after just two minutes when a gale blew down the goalposts. The rearranged fixture resulted in an 8-2 win for Darwen.

Halifax Town did not play a single home League game between 14 December 1962 and 2 March 1963 – all were postponed due to frost, ice and/or snow.

After the arctic winter of the previous season, only six Football League matches were postponed during the 1947/48 campaign – a record!

Due to atrocious weather, the Scottish Cup tie between Inverness Thistle and Partick Thistle was postponed twenty-eight times during the 1978/79 season.

Age

International Level

In April 1879, James Prinsep, aged seventeen years 252 days, made his international debut for England. He remained England's youngest player at that level until Wayne Rooney, aged seventeen years 111 days, played his first game as a substitute against Australia in February 2003. Seven months later Rooney became England's youngest-ever goalscorer when he netted against Macedonia in September 2003, and at one stage (in June 2004) he held the record for being the youngest goalscorer in the European Championship finals, at eighteen years 236 days.

Stanley Matthews was forty-two years 103 days old when he played his last game for England against Denmark in May 1957. His international career spanned twenty-two years 228 days, from 29 September 1934 to 15 May 1957.

Billy Meredith played in his first international match for Wales on 16 March 1895 and his last on 15 March 1920 – a span of twenty-five years.

Samuel Johnston was only fifteen years 154 days old when he played for Ireland in their first international match v. England in 1882. The following week he scored his first international goal (v. Wales).

Premiership

Matthew Briggs became the youngest player to appear in the Premiership when he made his debut as a substitute for Fulham against Middlesbrough on 13 May 2007 at the age of 16 years, 65 days.

At the age of sixteen years 271 days James Vaughan of Everton became the Premiership's youngest-ever goalscorer when he found the net in the home game against Crystal Palace on 10 April 2005.

Goalkeeper John Burridge is the oldest player ever to appear in a Premiership game. He was forty-three years, four months and twenty-six days old when he lined up for Manchester City against Newcastle United in April 1995.

The youngest goalkeeper to appear in a Premiership match has been Neil Finn for West Ham United against Manchester City in January 1996. He was just seventeen years, three days old.

Football League

Ken Owen Roberts was fifteen years 157 days old when he made his League debut for Wrexham against Bradford Park Avenue in September 1951.

Albert Geldard had been a day older when he started his first match for Bradford against Millwall in September 1929.

Glyn Pardoe was fifteen years ten months old when he made his First Division bow for Manchester City at centre forward against Birmingham City in 1962.

Lee Holmes was fifteen years 268 days old when he made his League debut for Derby County on Boxing Day 2002. He thus became the club's youngest-ever debutant, beating Steve Powell who was introduced against Arsenal in October 1971 at the age of sixteen years, thirty-three days. Prior to that Steve's father, Tommy Powell, had made his debut for Derby as a sixteen-year-old on Christmas Day 1941.

David Byng was sixteen years twenty-one days old when he made his senior debut for Torquay United against Walsall in August 1993. He celebrated the occasion by scoring both goals in a 2-1 win.

Jason Dozzell (aged sixteen years, fifty-seven days) became the youngest First Division goalscorer when he found the net against Coventry City in 1984.

Gifton Noel-Williams – the first Watford player with a double-barrelled name – made his League debut for the Hornets on 28 September 1996 v. Shrewsbury Town at the age of sixteen years, 250 days. He then became the Hornets' youngest-ever goalscorer, aged sixteen years, 314 days, when he netted against Blackpool on 30 November that same year.

Ronnie Dix was only fifteen years, 180 days old when he scored for Bristol Rovers against Norwich City in a Third Division (South) game in March 1928.

Derek Forster became the Football League's youngest-ever goalkeeper when he made his First Division debut for Sunderland against Leicester City in August 1964 at the age of fifteen years, 185 days.

Neil McBain was fifty-one years, four months old when he played in goal for New Brighton against Hartlepool United in a Third Division (North) match in 1947 – a Football League record.

Stanley Matthews' professional playing career covered thirty-two years and ten months. He officially retired after playing in his last League game for Stoke City against Fulham a few days after his fiftieth birthday in February 1965. He had made his debut for Stoke against Bury on 19 March 1932.

Dixie Dean and Jimmy Greaves were both the same age – twenty-three years, 290 days – when each player scored his 200th League goal.

Joe Cockcroft was thirty-eight years of age when he made his First Division debut for Sheffield United in 1948.

Bob McGrory, left-back of Stoke City, appeared in all his side's forty-two League games in 1934/35 at the age of forty.

FA Cup

Defender Andy Awford, aged fifteen years, eighty-eight days, played for Worcester City against Boreham Wood in the qualifying round of the FA Cup in October 1987 – the youngest player ever to appear in the competition.

On 10 November 2007, Luke Freeman became the youngest player to appear in the FA Cup proper when he came on as a substitute for Gillingham against Barnet at the age of 15 years and 233 days.

Alick Jeffrey lined up against Aston Villa on his sixteenth birthday in January 1955.

In 1949 Stan Cullis became the youngest man to manage an FA Cup-winning team, leading Wolves to victory over Leicester City at the age of thirty-three years, 187 days.

Billy Hampson (born in August 1882), right-back for Newcastle United v. Aston Villa in 1924, and John Oakes (born in September 1905), centre half for Charlton Athletic v. Derby County in 1946, are, at forty, the oldest players ever to appear in an FA Cup final.

In 1969, at the age of nineteen, Peter Shilton, then of Leicester City, became the youngest goalkeeper to play in an FA Cup final (against Manchester City).

League Cup

Chris Woods became the youngest goalkeeper at eighteen years 125 days to play in a major Wembley cup final when he lined up for Nottingham Forest against Liverpool in the 1978 League Cup final.

On 1 October 2002, in a League Cup tie at Wrexham, Wayne Rooney, aged sixteen years 342 days, became the youngest goalscorer in Everton's history, beating Tommy Lawton's record of scoring on his debut at the age of seventeen years 130 days on 13 March 1937.

Foreign Bodies

The Santos duo of George Dorval and Pelé both made their international debuts for Brazil against Argentina in July 1957 at the ages of fifteen years, one month and sixteen years nine months respectively. Both players had already played at League level prior to that, Dorval perhaps starting as a fourteen-year-old and Pelé as a fifteen-year-old.

Age Gap

Trevor Francis scored four goals for Birmingham City against Bolton Wanderers as a sixteen-year-old in a Second Division match in February 1971.

Eamonn Collins of Blackpool was only fourteen years 323 days old when he made his debut for the Seasiders as a substitute against Kilmarnock in the Anglo-Italian Cup in September 1980.

Goalkeeper John Burridge holds the record for being both Darlington's and Scarborough's oldest League player. He played his last competitive game for Scarborough in the Autoglass Trophy v. Hull City in December 1996, aged forty-five.

In 1928/29, Halifax Town's regular goalkeepers were Bob Suter (aged forty-nine) and Howard Matthews (forty-five).

When Newcastle United signed Andy Cunningham from Rangers in January 1929 he was thirty-nine years of age. He later became the first player-manager of a First Division club.

Stoke have signed two players over forty – Tom Brittleton (forty-one) was recruited from Sheffield Wednesday in May 1920 and Stanley Matthews (forty-six) returned home from Blackpool in October 1961.

Michael Gilsken holds three off-the-field football records: in August 1957, at the age of eighteen, he became the youngest-ever director of a League club (Charlton Athletic); he became the London club's youngest chairman in May 1962, aged twenty-three; and two years later he became the youngest-ever member of the Football League Management Committee.

Coventry City had three thirty-seven-year-old players appear in their League side during the 2002/03 season – Vicente Engonga, Gary McAllister and Steve Walsh.

Asby FC (Sweden) fielded sixty-seven-year-old right-winger Karl Sjoeberg in an intermediate League game against Krona in 1966. Asby lost 19-0.

The two regular full-backs of First Division Birmingham City in 1937 – Cyril Trigg and Billy Hughes – were both seventeen-year-olds.

Several footballers aged forty and over have regularly appeared in League games. Among them: defender Billy Hampson (Newcastle United, 1920s); wingers Billy Meredith (Manchester City and United, up to the First World War), Stanley Matthews (Blackpool and Stoke City, 1950s), John Page (Merthyr Town, 1920s) and David Eyres (Oldham Athletic, 2004); goalkeepers Peter Shilton (Derby County, 1990s), Kevin Poole (Bolton Wanderers, 2004) and Eric Nixon (Sheffield Wednesday, retired in 2004).

Ghanaian striker Nil Odartey Lamptey, later to play for Aston Villa and Coventry City, scored on his League debut for Anderlecht at the age of sixteen in December 1990. He then netted in each of his next three games and in March 1991 became the youngest-ever scorer in a major European game.

Terry Neill captained Bangor at the age of seventeen and both Arsenal and Northern Ireland at twenty-one. He was chairman of the PFA at twenty-four, became player-manager of Hull City at twenty-eight, managed Spurs at thirty-three and Arsenal at thirty-six and quit the game at forty-one.

Harry Kinghorn (trainer) was forty-eight years of age when he was forced into action by Bournemouth against Brentford in March 1929.

The former Port Vale, West Bromwich Albion, Crystal Palace and England international centre forward Ronnie Allen played in a friendly for WBA against Cheltenham Town in May 1995 at the age of sixty-six years, 115 days.

In August 1961, Sylvester Bicketon of Padiham near Burnley had a trial for Accrington Stanley – he was seventy-one.

In 2002, former Labour MP Michael Foot was given a squad number by Plymouth Argyle – at the age of ninety.

Appearances

Internationals

Goalkeeper Peter Shilton played in a record 125 full international matches for England over a twenty-year period from 1970.

Pat Jennings won 119 caps for Northern Ireland (1964-1986), Kenny Dalglish 102 for Scotland (1971-1986), Neville Southall 92 for Wales (1982-1997) and Steve Staunton 102 for the Republic of Ireland (1988-2002).

Other leading international cap winners include Mohamed Al-Deayea (Saudi Arabia) with a record 181 (at 2008), Claudio Suarez (Mexico) 177, Hossam Hassan (Egypt) 169, Martim Reim (Estonia) 156 and Lothar Matthius (Germany) 150.

Premiership

Wayne Bridge set a new record in January 2003 by appearing in 112 consecutive Premiership matches for Southampton without being substituted.

Frank Lampard made his 150th consecutive appearance for Chelsea in September 2005.

Welsh international midfielder Gary Speed holds the record for most appearances in the Premiership – amassing 535 between 1992 and 2008. David James has made over 530 and Ryan Giggs almost 520.

Football League

Peter Shilton made a record 1,005 League appearances while serving with ten different clubs between 1966 and 1996. He made over 100 for five of them: Leicester City (286), Stoke City (110), Nottingham Forest (202), Southampton (188) and Derby County (175). All told, he played in 1,390 first-class matches.

Harold Bell holds the record for most consecutive League appearances. Between 1946 and 1955 he lined up in 401 Third Division (North) games for Tranmere Rovers. He appeared in 574 of that club's first 582 post-Second World War League matches in thirteen seasons.

Over a period of eight seasons – 1952/53 to 1959/60 inclusive – centre forward Ray Straw appeared in all six divisions of the Football League. He played, in turn, for Derby County in the First, Second and Third (North) Divisions and for Coventry City in the Third (South), the newly formed Fourth Division and then the Third Division.

In 1961 goalkeeper Chic Brodie made consecutive appearances in the Fourth, First and Third Divisions for Aldershot, Wolves and Northampton Town respectively.

Jim Robertson played in the First, Second and Third Division (South) in that order in season 1937/38 when representing Huddersfield Town, Newcastle United and Millwall.

Midfielder Tony Gough played in his first League game in April 1959 for Bristol Rovers. His second came eleven years and 121 days later for Swindon Town in August 1970.

The versatile Jack Taylor is the only Everton player to have made 100 consecutive appearances from his debut. From 5 September 1896 to 24 March 1899 he completed a total of 122.

Full-back Stan Lynn was the only player to appear in twenty consecutive Football League seasons immediately following the Second World War (1946/47 to 1965/66 inclusive), doing so for Accrington Stanley, Aston Villa and Birmingham City.

Portsmouth in 1926/27, Huddersfield Town in 1952/53 and Aston Villa (Champions) in 1980/81, had seven ever-presents in their League sides during the seasons stated. Liverpool had five in 1965/66 when they also won the championship.

Ronnie Allen (with Port Vale, West Bromwich Albion and Crystal Palace) played – and scored – in nineteen consecutive post-Second World War campaigns (1946/47 to 1964/65). He also appeared and scored for Port Vale from April 1945 and in season 1945/46, thus making it twenty-one seasons in all.

Stanley Matthews' League career spanned twenty-seven seasons: from 1931/32 to 1938/39 and 1946/47 to 1964/65.

Neil McBain played his first League game in 1914 for Ayr United and his last thirty-three years later with New Brighton in 1947. He lost four seasons due to the First World War and did not play at all from 1939 until being called out in an emergency by the Rakers in 1947 at the age of fifty-one.

Billy Meredith played his first League game in 1894 and his last in 1924. He lost four of those thirty years due to the First World War.

Left-back George Mulholland made a record 231 consecutive League appearances for Bradford City between August 1953 and September 1958. With FA Cup games added, his overall tally was 246.

John Ruggiero played in all four divisions of the Football League in the space of seventeen games in the 1970s, serving with Workington (Fourth Division), Stoke City (Second Division), Brighton & Hove Albion (Second Division) and Portsmouth (Third Division). He later played for Chester (Third Division).

Only Ernie Butler appeared in all eighty-four League games for Portsmouth during their successive championship-winning seasons of 1948/49 and 1949/50.

Centre forward Harry Stapley is the only amateur to have played in every League match for a club in one complete season, doing so for Glossop in their Second Division campaign of 1910/11 (38 appearances).

England World Cup winner Alan Ball made over 100 League appearances for four different clubs: Blackpool, Everton, Arsenal and Southampton.

Goalkeeper John Wheeler, full-backs Ron Staniforth and Laurie Kelly and half-backs Bill McGarry, Don McEvoy and Len Quested played together in all of Huddersfield Town's forty-two Second Division matches in 1952/53. Including two FA Cup ties and two First Division fixtures at the start of the 1953/54 campaign, the same defensive formation lined up in a total of forty-eight competitive matches, a record.

FA Cup

Raich Carter was the only player to appear in an FA Cup-winning team either side of the Second World War – for Sunderland in 1937 and Derby County in 1946. Willie Fagan played for Preston in the 1937 final and for Liverpool in the 1950 final and was a loser both times.

Dave Mackay appeared in 36 FA Cup matches for Tottenham Hotspur and was on the losing side only three times. He gained three winners' medals, in 1961, 1962 and 1967.

Blackpool goalkeeper George Farm did not miss an FA Cup game between 1949 and 1961, making 47 appearances in total and playing in three finals, winning in 1953.

Luton Town and Nottingham Forest, FA Cup finalists in 1959, retained unchanged teams throughout the competition.

Roy Bentley appeared in seven FA Cup semi-finals with three different clubs and was never on the winning side. He was a loser with Newcastle United (v. Charlton Athletic) in 1947, with Chelsea (v. Arsenal) in replays in both 1950 and 1952 and with Fulham (v. Manchester United), also in a replay, in 1958.

European

Defender Bill Foulkes appeared in all of Manchester United's first forty-five European matches from 1955 to 1968, eventually playing in 52 out of a possible 58 while with United.

Manchester United's Ryan Giggs and Gary Neville have made more appearances in competitive European games than anyone else, with 100 and 99 respectively. They are closely followed by Raul of Real Madrid.

In September 2005, Paolo Maldini (AC Milan) set a new appearance record in Italy's Serie A by playing in his 571st game.

General

Besides his 931 Football League appearances, Tony Ford, who served with Grimsby Town, Sunderland, Stoke City (two spells), West Bromwich Albion, Bradford City, Scunthorpe United, Mansfield Town and Rochdale between 1975 and 2002, also played in 135 cup games and twice represented England at 'B' level. In all, he amassed 1,069 competitive appearances and played against more than 100 different clubs in the Football League.

Goalkeeper David Seaman made 1,020 senior appearances at club and international level up to the end of the 2002/03 season. His tally included 712 in the Premiership and Football League, 81 in the FA Cup, 73 in Europe, 59 in the League Cup and 91 for England (75 full caps).

Between 1903 and 1922, West Bromwich Albion and England full-back Jesse Pennington appeared in 540 first-class matches (League, FA Cup, Charity Shield, internationals, inter-League trials etc) and never scored a goal. He made his first and last League appearance for Albion against the same team, Liverpool.

Ian Callaghan appeared in ninety-two successive cup matches for Liverpool in various competitions. Clubmate Emlyn Hughes played in sixty-two FA Cup games in a row and in seventy-five out of seventy-six European encounters.

Roger Hunt (Liverpool and England) appeared in eighteen matches at Wembley and was never on the losing side. He helped Liverpool win the FA Cup in 1965 and England lift the World Cup twelve months later.

Bobby Charlton appeared in five major cup finals: the FA Cup in 1957, 1958 and 1963, the World Cup in 1966 and the European Cup in 1968. Including replays and two-legged encounters, he also appeared in twenty-eight various cup semi-finals as well as playing in forty-nine matches at Wembley: forty-four for England, four for Manchester United and once for the Three v. the Six in the Common Market representative game.

Three Sproson footballers – Roy, his brother Jess and his son Phil – collectively amassed 1,380 first-team appearances for Port Vale between 1940 and 1989.

When Terry Wollen and John Trollope started their full-back partnership with Swindon Town in the early 1960s, they had a combined age of thirty-four years three months. Wollen retired before he was twenty-one but Trollope went on to appear in well over 850 games for the Robins, quitting at the age of thirty-seven.

Arthur Wood enjoyed a run of 235 consecutive League and cup appearances for Leyton Orient from 3 September 1921 to 4 December 1926. He missed the next game against Blackpool and Orient lost 6-0.

Only three players have appeared in over 300 first-class matches for two different clubs – Stanley Matthews (Stoke City and Blackpool), Billy Meredith (Manchester City and Manchester United) and Alan Mullery (Spurs and Fulham).

Peter Swan appeared in 301 senior games for Sheffield Wednesday and never scored a goal. In 1973 he was transferred to Bury and netted after just ninety-five seconds of his debut for the Shakers.

International striker Andy Gray appeared in a major cup final for four different clubs: Dundee United (Scottish Cup), Aston Villa and Wolves (League Cup) and Everton (FA Cup and European Cup-Winners' Cup).

Full-back Phil Neal reached two personal milestones when Liverpool played Manchester United in April 1983. It was his 400th consecutive appearance for the Merseysiders and the 700th senior appearance of his career.

Top Football League
Appearance-makers (750+)

1,005	Peter Shilton	(1966-1997)
931	Tony Ford	(1975-2002)
824	Terry Paine	(1957-1977)
795	Tommy Hutchison	(1965-1991)
790	Neil Redfearn	(1982-2004)
782	Robbie James	(1973-1994)
777	Alan Oakes	(1959-1984)
774	Dave Beasant	(1797–2003)
770	John Trollope	(1960-1980)
764	Jimmy Dickinson	(1946-1965)
763	Stuart McColl	(1982–2004)
761	Roy Sproson	(1950-1972)
760	Mick Tait	(1975-1997)
758	Ray Clemence	(1966-1987)
758	Billy Bonds	(1964-1988)
757	Pat Jennings	(1963-1986)
757	Frank Worthington	(1966-1988)

Scottish League Appearance Records

Graeme Armstrong holds the record with 909 appearances in Scottish League football (1975-2001). His clubs included Meadowbank Thistle and Stirling Albion.

Allan Ball appeared in 731 League games for Queen of the South (1963-1982); goalkeeper Jim Gallagher made 642 between 1979 and 1992 and Jim Fallon played in 620 games for Clydebank (1968-1986)

David Narey's record of 612 League appearances for Dundee United covered twenty-one years (1973-1994) and Bobby Ferrier's total of 626 for Motherwell (1918-1937) is also a club record.

Other players with 500+ League appearances to their credit include Willie Miller (Aberdeen) 556, Ross Cavan (Queen's Park) 532, Paul Joaquin (Airdrieonians) 523, David Clarke (East Fife) 517, Gary Mackay (Hearts) 515 and Matt McPhee (Stirling Albion) 504.

Celtic's record appearance-maker in League football is Billy McNeill with 486 while the Rangers' mantle belongs to John Greig with 496.

Attendances

Premiership

Manchester United set a new average home League attendance record for a season in 1999/2000 (58,017), 2000/01 (67,544), 2001/02 (67,586), 2002/03 (67,630), 2003/04 (67,641), 2004/05 (67,871), 2005/06 (68,765) and 2006/07 (75,826).

The lowest attendance in the Premiership so far has been 3,039 for the Wimbledon v. Everton encounter in January 1993.

The highest Premiership crowd so far has been 76,098 for the Manchester United v. Blackburn Rovers clash at Old Trafford on 31 March 2007.

A Premiership crowd figure of 39,339 was officially declared at seven of Aston Villa's home games during the 1996/97 season.

Football League

The record for the biggest League crowd in England is 83,260 for the Manchester United v. Arsenal First Division encounter at Maine Road on 17 January 1948.

Blackpool allowed spectators in for free to watch their home Football League game with Swansea City in January 1994. The official attendance was recorded as 7,080, and is believed to be the highest for a non-paying competitive game in England.

Only thirteen people paid for admission to see the Stockport County v. Leicester League game on 7 May 1921. The fixture was staged at Old Trafford, Manchester, Stockport's ground having been closed by the Football League following crowd incidents. The match itself kicked off in late afternoon, following the Manchester United v. Derby County encounter that had been attended by 10,000 fans, of whom around 1,500 remained inside the ground to see the next match, having already paid.

Both League games between Lincoln City and Wrexham in 1976/77 attracted the same attendance: 7,753.

Stockport County's home games against Grimsby Town and Workington, in February and March 1971, attracted the same attendance: 1,777.

WAYNE

In season 1972/73 Workington's average home League attendance was just 1,436 (twenty-three Fourth Division games) – the lowest on record for any club since the First World War.

When Huddersfield Town won the First Division championship three seasons running – 1923-1926 – the average League attendance at Leeds Road over that period (sixty-three matches) was just 19,000.

Aston Villa averaged a Third Division-record 31,923 at their twenty-three home League games in 1971/72, making them the thirteenth-best-supported team in the entire country.

When Luton Town reached the 1959 FA Cup final (where they were beaten by Nottingham Forest) their average home League gate was 19,872, the lowest in the First Division.

On 29 August 1931, a crowd of 6,974 saw Rochdale play Accrington Stanley. Not far away, only 3,507 fans saw Manchester United take on Southampton at Old Trafford.

FA Cup

The world's first six-figure soccer crowd – 110,802 – assembled inside London's old Crystal Palace ground for the 1901 FA Cup final between Tottenham Hotspur and Sheffield United.

A fifth round FA Cup tie between Everton and Liverpool in March 1967 attracted an overall crowd of 105,000 – 64,831 spectators assembled at Goodison Park and there were 40,169 at Anfield where the game was transmitted live on closed-circuit TV.

The last 'official' 100,000 attendance on an England soccer ground was at Wembley Stadium for the 1985 FA Cup final between Manchester United and Everton.

A record crowd of 61,315 attended the Wolves v. Liverpool fifth round FA Cup tie at Molineux in February 1939. In February 1952, the Liverpool v. Wolves fourth round tie produced a record Anfield crowd of 61,905.

Scotland

A crowd of just twenty-nine watched the Scottish League Cup tie between Clydebank and East Stirling on 31 July 1999 – the lowest on record for a competitive game in the UK.

There were eighty spectators present at the Meadowbank Thistle v. Stenhousemuir clash on 22 December 1979 – one of the lowest on record for a Scottish League game.

By contrast, a crowd of 118,730 saw the Rangers v. Celtic Old Firm League derby at Ibrox Park in January 1939 – a record in the competition.

There was a record aggregate attendance of 265,725 for the Scottish Cup final and replay between Rangers and Morton in April 1948. A crowd of 131,975 watched the first game at Hampden Park and 133,750 attended the replay at the same venue.

European

A crowd of 136,505 attended Leeds United's European Cup semi-final showdown with Celtic at Hampden Park in April 1970 – a European record.

The 1960 European Cup final between Real Madrid and Eintracht Frankfurt at Hampden Park was witnessed by 135,076 spectators while the European final of two years earlier between Real Madrid and Fiorentina attracted a crowd of 124,124 to Real's home ground, the Bernabeu Stadium.

The only six-figure crowd for a European game in England (100,000) saw Manchester United beat Benfica 4-1 at Wembley in the European Cup final of 1968.

The lowest European Cup final crowd has been 22,897 for the replay of the 1974 showdown between Bayern Munich and Atletico Madrid in Brussels.

The record crowd for a Fairs Cup/UEFA Cup final is 93,267 for the Real Madrid v. Videotan second-leg clash at the Bernabeu Stadium in 1985.

A combined crowd figure of 150,098 saw the two legs of the Napoli v. Stuttgart UEFA Cup final of 1989: 83,107 in Italy and 66,991 in Germany.

By contrast a combined total of just 42,145 spectators attended the two legs of the 1978 final between Bastia and PSV Eindhoven.

The biggest attendance at a European Cup-Winners' Cup final was 100,554 for the Barcelona v. Standard Liege confrontation at the Nou Camp Stadium (Barcelona) in 1982. A crowd of 99,230 saw West Ham United beat TSV 1860 Munich in the 1965 final at Wembley.

Only 3,000 fans saw the 1964 Cup-Winners' Cup final between Sporting Lisbon and MTK Budapest in Brussels – the lowest on record for a major European final.

International

The biggest crowd ever to watch a football match is 199,850, at the giant Maracana Stadium in Rio de Janeiro for the Brazil v. Uruguay World Cup final in July 1950.

The biggest international crowd in Great Britain – 149,547 – packed into Hampden Park, Glasgow to witness the Scotland v. England clash in April 1937.

A record Second World War crowd of 133,128 saw Scotland play England at Hampden Park in April 1944. A year later there was an attendance of 132,956 for the same fixture at the same venue and 139,468 fans packed into the Glasgow stadium to witness the Victory International between Scotland and England in April 1946.

Crowd Talk

A crowd of 91,708 saw the pre-season friendly between Celtic and Tottenham Hotspur at Hampden Park on 5 August 1967.

In 1946/47, over 2.2 million people passed through the turnstiles at Maine Road, home of Manchester City. Both City and Manchester United played their home League games there that season. The FA Cup semi-final (Burnley v. Liverpool) and the Rugby League Challenge Cup final were also staged there.

The record attendance for a Southern League game is 29,786 for the QPR *v.* Plymouth Argyle encounter at Park Royal, London, on Christmas Day 1907.

Because of a snowstorm, only one fan paid to watch the Malfetta *v.* Martina Franca League game in Italy in 1962. At the game's end both sets of players lined up and cheered the spectator.

In 1998, Flamengo, one of Brazil's top teams, lost seven League games in a row and for the last of these matches there were only 791 fans inside the giant Maracana Stadium. Utterly disappointed, Kleber Liete, the club's president, decided that all spectators who attended the next game would get their money back if Flamengo lost. Over 52,000 supporters assembled inside the ground and, after leading twice, Flamengo then had two players sent off and lost the fixture 3-2. Thus poor old Mr Liete was a sick man after the final whistle with an awful lot of refunds to pay out!

Benefits & Testimonials

Goalkeeper Jimmy McLaren, with Bradford City, Leicester City and Watford between 1922 and 1939, and outside left Tommy Urwin, with Middlesbrough, Newcastle United and Sunderland between 1915 and 1935, both received three benefits.

The former West Bromwich Albion player Tony Brown also had three testimonials: in 1974 when still a player with WBA; in 1981 when registered with Torquay United; and another via WBA in 1999 when the Jamaican World Cup team visited The Hawthorns.

The first all-black team to play in a testimonial match did so at The Hawthorns, West Bromwich in 1979 when Cyrille Regis's XI played Len Cantello's XI.

Captains

On 11 June 2003, Michael Owen, winning his fiftieth cap, became England's youngest-ever captain at senior level when he led his country to a 2-1 win over Slovakia at the age of twenty-three years, 181 days.

Martin Buchan was twenty-one when he skippered Aberdeen to victory in the Scottish Cup final of 1970. Seven years later he led Manchester United to FA Cup final glory over Liverpool.

Barry Venison became the youngest player to skipper a Wembley cup final team when, at the age of twenty, he led Sunderland against Norwich City in the Milk Cup final of 1985.

David Nish of Leicester City is the youngest player to skipper an FA Cup final side (against Manchester City in 1969). He was twenty-one years of age.

Lee Cattermole captained Middlesbrough against Fulham in 2006 at the age of 18 years and 47 days, perhaps the youngest skipper in the Premiership.

Three England captains have played for Scunthorpe United – Kevin Keegan and Ray Clemence (football) and Ian Botham cricket).

George Mason captained Coventry City on and off for seventeen years between 1935 and 1952. He was skipper for thirteen consecutive seasons.

Centre half Frank Moss captained both Aston Villa (in the FA Cup final) and England (against Scotland) at Wembley in 1924.

Franz Beckenbauer is the only player to captain World Cup and European Cup-winning sides in the same year – West Germany and Bayern Munich in 1974.

Reginald Foster is the only man to have captained England at both cricket and football.

The respective captains in the Home International at Ninian Park in February 1924 – Fred Keenor (Wales) and Jimmy Blair (Scotland) – were both from the host club, Cardiff City.

Shirley Abbott captained Portsmouth for ten years from 1913 to 1923.

Championships

Three teams – Huddersfield Town (1923-1926), Arsenal (1932-1935) and Liverpool (1981-1984) – each achieved a hat-trick of League Championship triumphs. Manchester United followed with a hat-trick of Premiership titles in 1998-2001.

Rangers won a record fiftieth Scottish League title in 2002/03.

Liverpool have won a record eighteen League Championships – the first in 1901, the last in 1990. They have also finished runners-up on eleven occasions.

Chelsea won the League title in 1955 and fifty years later were crowned Premier League Champions for the first time.

Birmingham City, Luton Town and Rotherham finished the 1954–55 season level on points (54) at the top of the Second Division. The Blues won the title on goal-average.

Cricketer-Footballers

In 1964, Jim Standen won an FA Cup winners' medal with West Ham United and a County Championship medal with Worcestershire

Both Willie Watson and Ken Taylor were born in the West Riding of Yorkshire. They both played for Huddersfield Town's senior side and also appeared in the County Championship for Yorkshire as well as opening the batting for England in Test matches. After retiring both men became cricket coaches in South Africa.

Chris Balderstone was the first player to appear in a county cricket match and a Football League game on the same day, doing so in September 1975 for Leicestershire and Doncaster Rovers respectively.

Eric Houghton made his first-class cricket debut for Warwickshire CCC in 1946 just as he was starting his twentieth season as a footballer with Aston Villa.

Five footballers have appeared on the left wing with London-based Football League clubs and also played Test cricket for England. They are: Les Ames (Clapton Orient), Johnny Arnold (Fulham), Lawrie Fishlock (Millwall), Bill Edrich (Spurs) and Denis Compton (Arsenal).

Dual Internationals

Compton appeared in 78 Test matches, his first in 1937 versus New Zealand at The Oval. He played football in one Victory International and in 11 wartime internationals.

Others who represented England in both sports include Andy Ducat (Arsenal, Aston Villa and Fulham/Surrey); Reginald E. Foster (Oxford University/Worcestershire), Charles Burgess Fry (Corinthians and Southampton/Sussex and Hampshire), Leslie H. Gay (Old Brightonians/Cambridge University), William Gunn (Notts County/ Nottinghamshire), Harold T.W. Hardinge (Sheffield United/Kent), Patsy Hendren (Manchester City, Coventry City and Brentford/Middlesex), the Hon. Alfred Lyttelton (Old Etonians, Hagley and Cambridge University/Worcestershire and Middlesex, later president of the MCC), Harry Makepeace (Everton/Lancashire), Arthur Milton (Arsenal/Gloucestershire), John Sharp (Aston Villa and Everton/ Lancashire and Herefordshire) and Willie Watson (Sunderland and Huddersfield Town/Yorkshire).

Reginald Foster (see also under Captains) played in five full England internationals at football and in eight Test matches. He scored 9,076 runs for Worcestershire between 1899 and 1912. In his best innings, in 1903/04, he hit 287 for England against Australia.

Debuts

Football League

Centre half Charlie Davies is the only player in history who was with three clubs when each made its Football League debut: he was with Torquay United in 1927, York City in 1929 and Mansfield Town in 1931.

Without any other senior first-class experience as a player, Paul Wilson, youth team coach at Scunthorpe United, made his Football League debut for the club at the age of thirty-six years, 151 days in 1996.

Charlie Sutcliffe made his Football League debut for Rotherham County against South Shields in October 1920 – some thirty-one years after his brother, John W. Sutcliffe, had made his League bow for Bolton Wanderers in November 1889. Both were goalkeepers.

When defender Irving Rhodes netted from a free-kick for Rotherham United against Hartlepool United in March 1937, he became the first full-back to score on his League debut.

Norman Young joined Aston Villa in 1925. Ten years later, in 1935, he finally made his League debut against Preston North End.

Joe Cockroft was thirty-eight when he made his First Division debut for Sheffield United in 1948 while Andy Cunningham was thirty-eight years three days old when he made his League debut for Newcastle United in February 1929.

Terry Francis was only nineteen when he scored a hat-trick on his Football League debut for Hartlepool United v. Bradford Park Avenue in November 1963.

Ray Treacy scored on his League debut for West Bromwich Albion against Sunderland in October 1966 and after returning to The Hawthorns he scored on his second debut against Derby County in September 1976.

George Hilsdon scored five goals when making his Football League debut for Chelsea against Glossop (Second Division) in September 1906.

Among the players who have scored four goals on their League debuts are: Archie Gardiner for Leicester City v. Portsmouth in 1934, Tom Hall for Rotherham v. Wigan Borough in 1927, Fred Howard for Manchester City v. Liverpool in 1913, John Shepherd for Millwall v. Leyton Orient in 1952 and Ron Turnbull for Sunderland v. Portsmouth in 1947.

Ian Lawson scored four goals when making his senior debut in an FA Cup tie for Burnley against Chesterfield in 1957.

Signed from Torquay United, Colin Lee scored four goals when making his first appearance for Spurs in a 9-0 home League win over Bristol Rovers in October 1977.

Alf 'Nobby' Bentley, signed from Bolton Wanderers, scored four goals on his debut for West Bromwich Albion against Burnley in September 1913.

Goalkeeper Andy Donnelly joined Celtic in 1978 and it took him ten years before he finally made his senior debut – for Torquay United.

League Cup

Ralph Brown made his debut for Aston Villa in the first leg of the 1960/61 League Cup final v. Rotherham United. It was his only appearance for the club and he gained a winners' tankard.

John Boyle made his first-team debut for Chelsea against Aston Villa in a League Cup semi-final in January 1965. He scored the winning goal and went on to gain a winners' medal in the final.

Danny Campbell made his senior debut for West Bromwich Albion in the first leg of the 1966 League Cup final v. West Ham – and he too was on the winning side after an aggregate victory.

Debutant Simon Stainrod scored all of Aston Villa's goals in a 4-0 League Cup win over Exeter City in September 1985.

International

Hamish McAlpine made his debut for Scotland at Under-23 level against East Germany in October 1982 – at the age of thirty-four.

Named as England's reserve, centre forward Stan Mortensen made his international debut for Wales in a wartime game against his own country in September 1943 when he came on as a substitute for injured half-back Ivor Powell.

Theo Walcott became England's youngest-ever hat-trick hero when he netted three times against Croatia in 2008. He was almost 19 years and six months old.

Debut Day

Cyrille Regis scored on his debut for West Bromwich Albion in five different competitions in 1977 and 1978: Central League, League Cup, First Division, FA Cup and Tennent-Caledonian Cup.

1970s/80s striker David Johnson scored on his first appearance in the Football League, the FA Cup, the League Cup, the European Cup and for England (against Wales). He also became the first player to score for Everton against Liverpool and for Liverpool against Everton.

John Dyet scored eight goals when making his first-class debut for King's Park v. Forfar Athletic in a Scottish League Division Two game in January 1930. King's won 12-2.

Freddy Ady was only 14 years of age when he made his debut for the American-based club DC United v. San Jose Earthquakes in April 2004.

Barnsley's Reuben Nobe-Lazarus, aged 15 years and 45 days, became the Football League's youngest-ever player when he made his debut as a substitute v. Ipswich Town in October 2008.

Johnnie Mullington scored all of Macclesfield's goals when making his debut in an 8–0 win over Witton Albion in May 1963.

Defeats

Manchester United suffered 12 successive First Division defeats at the start of the 1930/31 season.

Nelson lost every single away Third Division (North) League game in 1930/31, suffering 21 defeats and conceding 73 goals.

In 1972/73, Aston Villa were defeated six times when travelling to seaside resorts. They lost to Bournemouth, Brighton & Hove Albion, Plymouth Argyle and Torquay United in the League, succumbed to Southend United in the FA Cup and Blackpool in the League Cup.

Discipline

Premiership

Barry Ferguson (Blackburn) was shown two yellow cards *v*. Southampton in 2004 but was not sent-off.

Goalkeeper Tim Flowers of Blackburn Rovers was sent off after just twenty-seven seconds of the game with Leeds United in February 1995 – a Premiership record.

Liverpool's Finnish defender Sami Hyypia was dismissed after four minutes during the away game with Manchester United in April 2003. United won 4-0 to register their biggest win over the Merseysiders for fifty years.

Newcastle United had three players sent off during their home game with Aston Villa in April 2005, two of them – Bowyer and Dyer – for fighting each other.

Football League

Ipswich Town beat Sheffield Wednesday 2-0 in a First Division game at Portman Road in December 1962 to move out of the bottom two. Later this fixture became the centre of a match-fixing scandal whereby, in January 1965, following criminal investigations, ten players (or ex-players) were subsequently sent to prison for conspiracy to defraud by fixing the result. Jimmy Gauld (the 'ringleader') was sentenced to four years' imprisonment with £5,000 costs while three Sheffield Wednesday players – David 'Bronco' Layne, Tony Kay and Peter Swan – all received four-month sentences.

The quickest sending off in Football League history is zero seconds: Walter Boyd (Swansea City) being the culprit at Darlington on 23 November 1999 (as a substitute).

A total of 73 yellow and four red cards were issued in twelve League games involving Chelsea and Leeds United up to November 2001.

Wrexham's Ambrose Brown was sent off after just twenty seconds of his side's away League game at Hull on Christmas Day 1936.

Notts County had nine players booked during a League game in December 1983.

The first manager to be sent off in a League game was Ronnie Rooke, as player-manager of Crystal Palace v. Millwall in October 1949.

Dixie McNeill (Wrexham) was sent off waiting to take a penalty kick against Charlton Athletic on 19 January 1980. Before the referee gave the signal for him to take the kick, in frustration, he belted the ball into the crowd and was immediately dismissed. Mick Vinter stepped up to score from the spot to earn Wrexham a 3-2 win.

The lowest number of sendings-off in one complete League season since 1919 (when the 42-match programme was introduced for the top two divisions) is five in 1947/48. The 50 mark was reached for the first time in 1966/67.

Defender Kevin Muscat (Millwall) and goalkeeper Paddy Kenny (Sheffield United) were both sent off in the tunnel at half-time of a Championship League game in December 2004.

Charlie George (Derby County) was sent off on the first and last days of the 1976/77 League season.

Over fifty red cards were shown to Arsenal players in the space of seven years: 1996-2003. The Gunners had topped the 60 mark by 2004.

A record number of 451 red cards were shown in League games in 2003–04 . . . 19 were handed out on one day – 13 December 2003.

Two players – Andreas Johansson, playing for Wigan v. Arsenal in 2006, and Keith Gillespie, playing for Sheffield United v. Reading in 2007, were sent-off after just 10 seconds of Premiership games.

In April 1986, the English brothers, Tony and Tommy, then of Colchester United, were both sent off in the League game against Crewe Alexandra at Gresty Road.

In 1988, Shrewsbury Town's Vic Kasule was booked against Crystal Palace for whistling a George Benson song when he should have been taking a corner!

Everton played Liverpool 120 times without a player ever being sent off. Then, in match number 121 – a League game in November 1979 – Terry McDermott (Liverpool) and Gary Stanley (Everton) both took early baths.

Defender Glen Keeley was sent off in his only game for Everton against Liverpool in November 1982.

Cup Competitions

Two players – Kevin Moran (Manchester United 1985) and Jose Antonio Reyes (Arsenal 2005) – have been sent off in FA Cup finals.

During a third round FA Cup tie against Maidstone United in January 1979, two Charlton Athletic players – Mike Flanagan and Derek Hales – were dismissed for fighting each other.

Giuseppe Lorenzo of Bologna was sent off just ten seconds into the Italian Serie 'A' game against Parma in December 1990.

Championship of the World

On 5 November 1967, Celtic, the European Cup holders, met Racing Club of Argentina, the South American Cup winners, in a decider for the 'Championship of the World' after the aggregate scores over two legs had finished level at 2-2, Celtic having won 1-0 in Glasgow and Racing 2-1 in Buenos Aires. The decider took place on a neutral ground in Montevideo, Uruguay, and what a heated battle it turned out to be! The game contained over sixty fouls and six players were sent off by the Paraguayan referee Rodolfo Perez Oserio. Basile (Racing) and Bobby Lennox (Celtic) were dismissed for fighting in the first half and they were followed by Jimmy Johnstone, John Hughes and

Bertie Auld (Celtic) and Rulli (Racing) after the break. Racing won 1-0. Celtic chairman Robert Kelly announced later that the club had fined all the players who had taken part in the game £250, saying, 'They were all in it together.'

Internationals

Jose Batista of Uruguay was dismissed after fifty-five seconds of his country's World Cup match *v*. Scotland in Mexico in 1986.

Antonio Rattin, captain of Argentina, became the first player to be sent off at Wembley, dismissed for arguing in the World Cup quarter-final tie with England in 1966.

Four Angola players were sent off and another taken off injured during an international match with Portugal in Lisbon in November 2001. The game was abandoned with twenty-two minutes remaining.

Wing half Alan Mullery (Tottenham Hotspur) was the first England player to be sent off in a full international, dismissed in the European Nations Cup semi-final against Yugoslavia in 1968.

Ray Wilkins was the first England player to be sent off in the World Cup, dismissed against Morocco in June 1986.

The entire Ecuador team (all eleven players) were sent off in an international match in 1978.

Trevor Hockey was the first player to be sent off in a full international match for Wales.

Johann Cruyff was suspended by the Dutch FA for twelve months after being sent off playing for Holland against Czechoslovakia in 1966. This was only his second full international appearance.

Bulgaria had three players sent off in the 1968 Olympic Games soccer final.

European Competitions

Leeds United midfielder Mick Bates was the first British player to be sent off twice in the same European competition, dismissed in the Fairs Cup against Partizan Belgrade in November 1967 and Dinamo Bucharest in November 1970.

Stoke City's substitute striker John Ritchie was sent off in a UEFA Cup clash with FC Kaiserslautern in 1972 after being on the pitch for just thirty-nine seconds.

Birmingham City had eight players sent off in Inter-Cities Fairs Cup matches between 1955 and 1961.

In Trouble

In December 2003, the Manchester United and England defender Rio Ferdinand was banned from all competitions for eight months, fined £50,000 and ordered to pay costs after being found guilty of missing a drug test three months earlier. An appeal (by Manchester United) failed as FIFA was happy with the final decision, which ran from January to September 2004.

Stranrear finished their League game with Airdrieonians in December 1974 with only seven players, four having been sent off. They lost 8-1.

A new record was set in 2003/04 when 451 players were shown red cards during Premiership and League games in England.

Ramon Moya, manager of CF Hospitalet, lost control of himself when his side scored a dramatic last-minute winner in a Spanish Second Division match in 1998 against CF Figueres and was sent off – for kissing a linesman!

The most sendings-off in one day is nineteen: all in the League on 13 December 2003.

Arsenal had three players sent off in four days at Turf Moor in 1967. Bob McNab was dismissed in a League Cup tie on 28 November and when the Gunners played Burnley in a First Division game on 2 December, both Peter Storey and Frank McLintock were ordered off.

In 1990/91, Nigel Pepper of York City was sent off three times against Darlington – in both Fourth Division games and in an FA Cup tie.

During a needle match in the early 1950s between two Algerian teams, Marengo and Blida, played at Blida, fighting broke out on the field and the referee sent off two Marengo players. They refused to leave the pitch, so the official stopped the game, at which point fighting started again. As a result the local police were called and one of them was struck by a Marengo player who was immediately arrested and detained in jail for three days. As a protest the whole municipal council of Marengo resigned.

Leicester Fosse centre forward Tommy Brown received an indefinite suspension in September 1901 for frequent breaches of club discipline.

Two Scottish international inside forwards were suspended in season 1964/65. Manchester United's Denis Law received a twenty-eight-day ban and missed three matches while Leicester's David Gibson was sidelined for five games despite only receiving a fourteen-day suspension.

In a match in Verviers, Belgium in 1951, when the referee failed to spot a blatant foul, the King's Attorney, Martin Van Dresse, who saw it, sent two gendarmes on to the pitch to question the offending player. The result led to a court case in which the footballer was fined £20 and given a long suspension while the referee was publicly lectured in court.

In 1963, two Darlington players – Bill Smith and John Duffy – were sent off for fighting each other during a reserve game at Halifax.

Eight players, four from each side, were sent off during the heated Uruguayan League game between Naçional and the Wanderers in Montevideo in 1965/66.

Ian Callaghan was booked for the first time in his career when playing in his 849th senior game for Liverpool in March 1978.

Three players from the Argentinian club Estudiantes were imprisoned by the country's President after an unruly World Club Championship clash with AC Milan.

Doncaster Rovers' midfielder David Harle was sent off three times in 1984/85 and once more the following season. During his career he received ten dismissals.

Kevin Keegan (Liverpool) and Billy Bremner (Leeds United) were sent off for fighting in the FA Charity Shield at Wembley in 1974.

Injured playing for Busc against Pecs in a club match in Hungary in 1968, Sandor Grasic passed remarks to the referee as he lay on the stretcher. The official reached for his notebook and as well as Grasic being carried off, he was also sent off.

It is believed that hard-nut defender Frank Barson was sent off more times than any other footballer during a career that spanned nineteen years (1911-1930). He was dismissed twelve times in League football, on six occasions in cup competitions and twice at other levels. It is understood that Barson was also booked at least once every season he played.

Winger Willie Johnston (Rangers, West Bromwich Albion, Vancouver Whitecaps, Birmingham City, Hearts and Scotland) was sent off seventeen times in senior games between 1967 and 1983.

George Best was sent off playing for Northern Ireland on 18 April 1970 and 18 October 1971 and in between times he was dismissed playing for Manchester United on 18 August 1970. I wonder if eighteen was his unlucky number?

Doug Fraser (Walsall) and Kenny Stephens (Bristol Rovers) were sent off for fighting during a League game in 1973. Five years earlier they had been teammates at West Bromwich Albion in the FA Cup semi-final win over Birmingham City.

Tottenham Hotspur did not have a player sent off in a senior game between 1928 and 1965. Not one Nottingham Forest player was dismissed between 1939 and 1971, nor a Leeds United player between 1922 and 1958, nor a Fulham player between 1938 and 1963. Surprisingly, it was Johnny Haynes who ended the Cottagers' fine run!

Doubling Up

Old Carthusians completed a unique double when they won the FA Amateur Cup in 1894, having lifted the FA (English) Cup in 1881.

In 1930/31, West Bromwich Albion won the FA Cup and gained promotion from the Second Division in the same season – a feat never achieved before or since.

Preston North End were the first team to complete the League and FA Cup double, doing so in 1888/89 when they played a total of 27 games, winning 23 (18 in the League), scoring 85 goals and conceding only 15 (all in the League).

When Aston Villa emulated North End's feat in 1896/97, they fulfilled 37 fixtures (26 of them victories) and scored 90 goals, conceding 44.

Since then Tottenham Hotspur, Arsenal, Liverpool and Manchester United have all won the coveted League and FA Cup double in England.

On Christmas Day 1935, Kettering Town won 9-1 away to Higham Town in the Northants League with Alex Linnell scoring four times. Kettering also won the return fixture on Boxing Day, this time by 20-3, Linnell netting seven goals – thus securing a record tally of 29 goals to complete the 'double'.

Draws
(Football League)

In season 1896/97, Darwen failed to register a single draw in 30 League games. They won 14 and lost 16.

Norwich City drew 23 of their 42 First Division League games in 1978/79 (10 at home, 13 away) while in the same season, Carlisle United drew 22 of their 46 Third Division matches.

Tottenham Hotspur have been involved in two 5-5 League draws: with Huddersfield Town in September 1925 and Aston Villa in March 1966. They led Villa 5-1 at one stage.

West Ham United also played out two 5-5 draws, both away, against Newcastle United in December 1960 and at Chelsea in December 1966.

Thirty years later, in October 1960, Charlton Athletic and Middlesbrough drew 6-6 in a Second Division fixture at The Valley – the last time this scoreline occurred.

Aston Villa played out goal-less draws in home games against Manchester United in August 1928 and Liverpool in September 1932. During the intervening four years they fulfilled 170 fixtures without a 0-0 draw – a Football League record.

Tranmere Rovers drew 11 home and away games (from a total of 22) in season 1970/71 – also a League record.

European Football

Chelsea beat the Luxembourg team Jeunesse Hautarange 23-0 on aggregate in the 1971/72 European Cup-Winners' Cup. The Blues won 13-0 at home and 10-0 away.

Benfica of Portugal beat Dudelauge of Luxembourg 18-0 on aggregate in a preliminary round of the European Cup in 1965.

Belgian club RSC Anderlecht were the first side to reach three successive European Cup-Winners' Cup finals

The first British side to play a competitive game in a major European club competition was Hibernian, who met Rot-Weiss Essen of Germany in the European Cup in September 1955.

Newport County went 302 minutes of European Cup-Winners' Cup football in 1986/87 without conceding a goal.

England were the first country to have three different winners of the European Cup-Winners' Cup: Tottenham Hotspur (1963), West Ham United (1965) and Manchester City (1971). Chelsea made it four (1972) and since then Everton (1985), Manchester United (1991), Arsenal (1994) and Chelsea again (1998) have all won the trophy.

Two English clubs – Tottenham Hotspur and Wolves – contested the first ever UEFA Cup final in 1971/72. Tottenham were the winners.

In April 1970, Derby County were fined £10,000 and banned from European competitions for a year following allegations of irregularities in the club's bookkeeping.

The Belgium international Josef Jurion (Anderlecht), whose goal knocked Real Madrid out of the 1961/62 European Cup, played in spectacles throughout his twenty-year career.

Gordon Smith was the first player to appear in the European Cup competition for three different clubs, all from Scotland: Hibernian (1955/56), Heart of Midlothian (1960/61) and Dundee (1962/63).

1-0 was the score in every European Cup final between 1978 and 1983.

Left-back Tommy Gemmill scored for Celtic in both the 1967 and 1970 European Cup finals.

French international Raymond Kopa played for Rheims against Real Madrid in the 1956 European Cup final and Real Madrid against his former club in the 1959 final.

Jose Altafini of AC Milan and Ruud van Nistelrooy of Manchester United share the record for scoring the most European Cup/Champions League goals in a season, with 14, in 1962/63 and 2002/03 respectively.

The record average attendance for one season of European Cup football was set in 1959/60: 50,545. The top average for the Champions League is the 45,529 (aggregate 1,202,289) recorded in 1993/94.

The biggest win in a European Cup match is 12-0 by Feyenoord (Holland) over RK Reykjavik (Iceland) in 1969. In the Champions League, Juventus beat Olympiakos of Greece 7-0 in December 2003.

Raul (Real Madrid) has scored most goals in European Cup/Champions League history. He has so far netted 63 (since 1995). Ruud van Nistelrooy has scored 60 (since 1998) and Andriy Shevchenko 57 (since 1994). Di Stefano (Real Madrid) hit 49 (1955–64).

Best European comeback: SV Werder Bremen were 3-0 down after thirty-three minutes at home to RSC Anderlecht of Belgium in the Champions League in December 1993. The Bundesliga side stormed back to win 5-3.

Barcelona claimed a record 11 successive wins in the Champions League in 2002/03.

Roy Maackay (Bayern Munich) has scored the fastest goal in the Champions League to date, netting after just 10 seconds play against Real Madrid on 7 March 2007.

Dutchmen Frank Rijkaard and Clarence Seedorf both gained three European Cup/Champions League winners' medals, the former in 1989 and 1990 with AC Milan and 1995 with Ajax, the latter in 1995 with Ajax, 1998 with Real Madrid and 2003 with AC Milan.

Real Madrid have appeared in a record twelve European Cup/Champions League finals. They have won the title on nine occasions to AC Milan's seven.

The Italian defender Paolo Maldini of AC Milan played in a record 171 competitive European matches between 1985 and 2008.

Liverpool's Bob Paisley is the most successful manager in the history of the European Cup, winning the trophy three times in 1977, 1978 and 1981.

FA Cup

Final Action

When Cardiff City beat Arsenal 1-0 in the 1927 FA Cup final (to take the trophy out of England for the first time) the all-important goal was scored by a Scotsman (Hughie Ferguson) past a Welsh 'keeper (Dan Lewis).

Preston North End lost three FA Cup finals after being in the lead: in 1937 (beaten by Sunderland), in 1954 (eclipsed by West Bromwich Albion) and in 1964 (defeated by West Ham).

Jim Forrest (with Blackburn Rovers in 1884, 1885, 1886, 1890 and 1891); Lord A.F. Kinnaird (with The Wanderers in 1873, 1877, 1878 and Old Etonians in 1879,

1882) and Charles Wollaston (with The Wanderers in 1872, 1873, 1876, 1877 and 1878) all gained five FA Cup winners' medals. Kinnaird played in nine of the first twelve finals – a record.

Joe Hulme appeared in five Wembley FA Cup finals – four with Arsenal (1927, 1930, 1932 and 1936) and one with Huddersfield Town (1922).

Dennis Wise is another five-final man – four at Wembley with Wimbledon (1988) and Chelsea (1994, 1997 and 2000) plus one at Cardiff's Millennium Stadium, as player-manager of Millwall (2004). Ryan Giggs of Manchester United has also played in five finals.

Johnny Giles also played in five final matches (six including a replay), for Manchester United in 1963 and for Leeds United in 1965, 1970 (twice including the replay at Old Trafford), 1972 and 1973.

Leicester City have appeared in four FA Cup finals and lost them all – in 1949, 1961, 1963 and 1969.

Harold Halse played for Manchester United, Aston Villa and Chelsea in FA Cup finals between 1909 and 1915.

The first player to wear the number twelve shirt in an FA Cup final was Eric Brook, outside left of Manchester City, in the 1933 contest with Everton. For this final the participating players were numbered 1-22.

Bury have recorded the biggest win in an FA Cup final, beating Derby County 6-0 in 1903.

The first man to appear in a winning FA Cup final team and then manage a winning team was Scotsman Peter McWilliam. He respectively collected medals with Newcastle United in 1910 and Tottenham Hotspur in 1921.

Newcastle United's FA Cup-winning team in 1910 contained nine full internationals. Lawrence and Low were the odd men out but they were capped the following year.

As a player Joe Smith was an FA Cup winner with Bolton Wanderers in 1923. Thirty years later he once more tasted cup glory, this time as manager of Blackpool, who defeated his former club 4-3 in the final.

Alan Mullery played in two FA Cup finals for two London clubs against two other London clubs: for Tottenham Hotspur v. Chelsea in 1967 and for Fulham v. West Ham United in 1975.

Blackburn Rovers beat the Scottish club Queen's Park in both the 1884 and 1885 FA Cup finals. On each occasion Rovers scored two goals and the marksmen were

WAYNE

the same – Brown and Forrest. Rovers won the trophy for the third time in 1886 and again Brown was a goalscorer.

The 1975 all-London FA Cup final between Fulham v. West Ham United featured twenty-three Englishmen and one Irishman, Jimmy Conway of Fulham being the odd man out.

The 1924 FA Cup final between Aston Villa and Newcastle United was the first all-ticket affair.

Wolves have played an FA Cup final on five grounds – more than any other club. The venues were the Kennington Oval, Fallowfield (Manchester), Crystal Palace, Stamford Bridge and Wembley Stadium. They also played in a play-off final at Cardiff's Millennium Stadium.

Tommy Johnson played for Manchester City against Bolton Wanderers in the 1926 FA Cup final and for Everton against Manchester City in the 1929 final. City lost both matches.

Defender David O'Leary played in FA Cup finals fifteen years apart – for Arsenal *v.* Ipswich Town in 1978 and for Arsenal *v.* Sheffield Wednesday in 1993.

Nottingham Forest winger Roy Dwight scored what proved to be the winning goal in the 1959 FA Cup final *v.* Luton Town but watched the presentation of the trophy from his hospital bed after being carried off with a broken leg. His uncle, Elton John, was chairman of Watford when they played in the 1984 final.

Cup Gossip

Birmingham, then the reigning Second Division champions, did not participate in the FA Cup in 1921/22 – the club secretary forgot to submit their entry form.

Nottingham Forest have played an FA Cup tie in four different countries – England (several times), Scotland (*v.* Queen's Park in Edinburgh, 1885), Ireland (*v.* Linfield, 1889) and Wales (*v.* Cardiff City, 1922 and Swansea Town, 1929).

Crystal Palace were drawn away in the third round of the FA Cup for a record tenth successive time in 1978/79.

Crewe Alexandra were the last amateur side to reach the semi-final of the FA Cup, losing to Preston North End 4-0 in February 1888.

Bradford City lost an FA Cup tie at Worksop Town in December 1955. Two days later City's reserve side won a Midland League game against the same opponents on the same ground.

Notts County did not beat another Football League team in the FA Cup between January 1958 and November 1970.

Newcastle United took the FA Cup with them on tour to South Africa in 1952. This was the first time the coveted trophy had left the British Isles.

The FA Cup semi-final between Queen's Park and Nottingham Forest in March 1885 was staged at the Merchiston Castle School Ground in Edinburgh.

Only one of London's major professional clubs – Brentford – has never appeared in an FA Cup semi-final.

Welsh international Roy Paul played in all twelve rounds of the FA Cup during his career, from two finals with Manchester City in the mid-1950s down to the first qualifying round with Worcester City.

Villa Park has staged the most FA Cup semi-final matches – in total fifty-three between 1901 and 2004.

In 1899, Arsenal took nine-and-a-half hours (five games, covering 570 minutes) to settle their third qualifying round FA Cup tie with Gillingham (then known as New Brompton).

Ronnie Starling played in semi-finals with four different clubs in nine years: Hull City 1930 (lost), Newcastle United 1932 (won), Sheffield Wednesday 1935 (won) and Aston Villa 1938 (lost).

Then, in 1924, Gillingham themselves took precisely the same length of time to finish an FA Cup tie with Barrow, while in January 1955 the Bury v. Stoke City third round encounter ran for nine hours twenty-two minutes before the Potters went through to meet Swansea. This tie was shorter than those above because the first replay at Stoke was abandoned eight minutes before the final whistle.

The first top division club to be ousted from the FA Cup via a penalty shoot-out was Manchester United, beaten 4-2 from the spot by Southampton at Old Trafford in February 1992.

Arsenal played seven FA Cup matches in London when winning the trophy in season 1949/50.

Manchester City played four post-Second World War semi-finals at Villa Park – in 1955, 1956, 1969 and 1981 – and won them all with a 1-0 scoreline.

The first FA Cup competition in 1871/72 attracted fifteen entries, three of whom scratched.

Blackburn Rovers hold the all-time record of consecutive FA Cup matches without defeat – 24 games from December 1883 to December 1886. They won the trophy three times during that period.

In 1873 Oxford University lost both the FA Cup final and the Boat Race on the same day.

Bournemouth are the only Football League club to have met and defeated three amateur sides in successive rounds of the FA Cup.

Manchester City have recorded the biggest away replay win in the FA Cup. After being held to a draw at Maine Road in 1968, they thrashed Reading 7-0 at Elm Park.

On their way to the 1966 final Everton went seven FA Cup games without conceding a goal.

Manchester United played 'home' FA Cup ties on the grounds of Huddersfield Town, Liverpool and Manchester City in the late 1940s.

Aldershot, Barnsley, Brentford, Bristol Rovers, Chelsea, Stoke City, Wrexham and York City all lost three FA Cup games in the same season, 1945/46 – when all rounds up to the semi-final stage were played over two legs.

Fulham are the only team to have beaten a team that went on to reach the FA Cup final in the same season. The Cottagers defeated Charlton Athletic 2-1 in a third round second leg clash in January 1946, when all rounds prior to the semi-final stage were played over two legs. Charlton won 4-3 on aggregate and went on to reach the final, where they lost to Derby County.

Jimmy Greenhoff scored in two semi-finals for two different teams on the same ground – Goodison Park – for Stoke City in 1972 and for Manchester United in 1979.

Between 1959 and 1968, Manchester United played a record fifteen away FA Cup games without defeat.

Preston North End played two successive away FA Cup ties on the same ground in 1948. They beat Manchester City 1-0 at Maine Road and then lost 4-1 to Manchester United, also at Maine Road following the closure of Old Trafford due to wartime bombing.

In 1970/71, Leeds United (top of the First Division) were sensationally knocked out of the FA Cup by Colchester United (ninety-second and last in the Football League).

In season 1932/33, Brighton & Hove Albion forgot to make the formal application for exemption from the qualifying rounds of the FA Cup so they had to play through four extra rounds beginning in October. They defeated, in the preliminary rounds, Shoreham 12-0, Worthing 7-1, Hastings & St Leonard's 9-0 and Barnet 4-0. They followed this up in the competition proper by knocking out Crystal Palace 2-1, Wrexham 3-2 (in a replay), Chelsea 2-1 and Bradford Park Avenue 2-1 before going out in round five to West Ham United 1-0 (in another replay). They played a total of eleven matches.

Notts County have competed in every FA Cup competition since 1877 – a record.

Neighbours Bolton Wanderers and Preston North End were paired together on five separate occasions in the FA Cup between 1958 and 1966.

The first FA Cup final to be broadcast on live radio was the 1927 clash between Arsenal and Cardiff City.

The first goal at Wembley was scored by David Jack for Bolton Wanderers against West Ham United in the 1923 FA Cup final.

Full-back Bert Turner was the first player to score for both sides in an FA Cup final – doing so for Charlton Athletic (his own club) and also registering an own goal for Derby County in 1946.

The first FA Cup tie to be staged on a Sunday was between Cambridge United and Oldham Athletic at The Abbey Stadium on 6 January 1974. A crowd of 8,479 witnessed the 2-2 draw.

The first FA Cup final to be televised in colour was that between West Bromwich Albion and Everton in 1968. This same final also saw the first substitute used – Dennis Clarke (wearing the number twelve shirt) replacing John Kaye in Albion's defence at the start of extra time.

The first substitutes to be named for an FA Cup final were Joe Kirkup (Chelsea) and Cliff Jones (Tottenham Hotspur) in 1967. Neither came on.

Before they gained entry to the Football League (in 1972) Hereford United created a record by qualifying for the FA Cup first round proper on twenty-one successive occasions.

Druids (from Ruabon) were the first Welsh club to enter the FA Cup.

Martin Buchan was the first player to captain Scottish (Aberdeen) and English (Manchester United) FA Cup-winning teams.

Wigan Athletic became the first non-League side to win an FA Cup tie on a Football League ground when they defeated Carlisle United in 1934/35.

Jimmy Scoular was the first player to appear in the FA Cup competition for different clubs in the same season, serving both Gosport Borough and Portsmouth in 1945/46. Stan Crowther followed him in 1957/58 when he starred for Aston Villa and then Manchester United.

The first floodlit game involving two League clubs took place later that same year (1955) when Darlington met Carlisle United in an FA Cup replay at St James' Park, Newcastle.

Brighton met Watford four seasons running in the FA Cup: 1924–25 to 1927–28. Six games were played in all.

It took 6 hours, 14 minutes for the first goal to be scored in the Crystal Palace v. Notts County FA Cup-tie in February 1924. County eventually got it in the second replay.

Family Connection

Brotherly Love

Five members of the Clarke family played professional football. Allan served with Walsall, Fulham, Leicester City, Leeds United and Barnsley; Derek with Walsall, Wolves, Oxford United, Leyton Orient and Carlisle United; Frank with Shrewsbury Town, Queens Park Rangers, Ipswich Town and Carlisle United; Kelvin with Walsall and Wayne with Wolves, Birmingham City, Everton, Leicester City, Manchester City, Shrewsbury Town, Stoke City and Walsall. Collectively they scored 323 goals in a combined total of 1,126 League appearances. Allan won 19 England caps and amazingly all five brothers were with clubs that suffered relegation!

Two of the Bambridge brothers, Arthur Leopold and Edward Charles, appeared together for England v. Wales in 1883 and v. Ireland in 1884. Another brother, Ernest Henry, had been capped earlier (1876).

Arthur and Harry Cursham of Notts County played together for England v. Scotland and Wales in season 1882/83.

The Old Carthusian brothers A.M. and P.M. Walters were full-back partners at international level for England in the 1880s and were followed by the Nottingham Forest duo of Frank and Fred Forman who played in the same England side in the 1890s.

The Charlton brothers, Jack and Bobby, helped England win the World Cup in 1966. Between them they won 141 full caps and for their respective clubs – Jack with Leeds United and Bobby with Manchester United and Preston North End – they amassed more than 1,500 League and cup appearances covering a period of twenty-five years.

Fritz and Ottmar Walter were World Cup winners in the same West German side (v. Hungary) in 1954.

Since then we had the Neville brothers, Gary and Phil, playing together for both Manchester United and England.

In 2007–08, Barnsley became the first non top-flight team to knock two high-flying Premiership clubs out of the FA Cup in successive rounds, beating Liverpool 2–1 at Anfield and Chelsea 1–0 at Oakwell.

In 1876, Frederick and Hubert Heron were FA Cup winners with the Wanderers and also appeared together for England v. Scotland.

In the 1890s, the Goodall brothers – John (Preston North End and Derby County) and his brother Archie (Derby County and Glossop) – won 24 international caps between them, John gaining 14 with England and Archie 10 with Ireland. They never opposed each other.

Brothers John and Samuel Jones played for Ireland against England and Wales in 1933 while their brother-in-law Bill Mitchell completed the half-back line against the Welsh.

Danny and Jackie Blanchflower played in the same Northern Ireland side in the mid-1950s, brothers John and Mel Charles starred together for Wales in fifteen internationals between 1955 and 1962 and the Allchurch brothers, Ivor and Len, played together in eight games for Wales between 1955 and 1963.

On 20 April 1955, a new record was set when two pairs of brothers played in the same side in an international match when John and Mel Charles and Ivor and Len Allchurch lined up for Wales against Northern Ireland.

Brothers Jack and Roger Doughty (Druids) scored seven goals between them as Wales beat Ireland 11-0 at Wrexham in 1888.

In 1967, Dave Hollins won his first cap for Wales and his brother John for England.

Dr Kevin O'Flanagan and his brother Michael occupied the right wing and centre forward positions respectively for Eire against England in Dublin in 1946.

David Shaw (Hibernian) and his brother Jack (Rangers) were full-back partners for Scotland against England and Switzerland in 1946.

Mario and Juan Evaristo appeared together for Argentina in the 1930s; Albert and Robert Koerner did likewise for Austria in the 1950s and so did three Abegglen brothers, Jean, Max and André ('Trello') for Switzerland in the 1930s.

There have been several instances of two sets of brothers playing together in the same Football League side: Frank and Fred Forman and Arthur and Adrian Capes starred for Nottingham Forest in 1896/97; Samuel and John Tonner and Thomas and Owen Williams likewise for Clapton Orient in 1921/22 and 1922/23; Peter and John Butler and Tony and Peter Bircumshaw turned out for Notts County in 1961/62; Cyril and Gilbert Beech or Cliff and Bryn Jones with Ivor and Len Allchurch did the same for Swansea Town in 1953/54 as did Ray and Pat Brady and Roger and Ian Morgan for QPR in 1964/65.

Swansea Town had four pairs of brothers on their professional staff in 1953/54: Colin and Alan Hole plus the brothers Beech, Jones and Allchurch (above).

Full-backs John, James and George Milburn were registered with Leeds United from 1935 to 1937. They each received a benefit cheque. Another brother, Stan, played for Chesterfield, Leicester City and Rochdale.

Brothers Mark and Bill Hooper partnered each other in Darlington's forward line after the First World War but only once did they both score in the same match – in a 4-0 home win over Rotherham County in October 1924.

In June 1952, brothers Jack and Frank Taylor, who were together at Wolves before the Second World War, both became League club managers, Jack at Leeds and Frank at Stoke. In season 1960/61 they both lost their jobs.

Brothers Mark and Steve Aizlewood both played for Newport County at the age of sixteen.

On 22 May 1967, Sheffield Wednesday transferred thirty-one-year-old goalkeeper Ron Springett to Queens Park Rangers where he replaced his twenty-one-year-old brother Peter, who moved to Hillsborough.

Ray Parry (Bolton Wanderers, Blackpool and Bury) and his brother Jack Parry (Derby County) both scored over a century of goals. Two other Parry brothers – Cyril and Glyn – also played football.

Three brothers – John and Bill Smith of Portsmouth and Septimus Smith of Leicester City – played in the 1934 FA Cup semi-final.

Right-winger Alan Moore, one of ten brothers, eight of whom played football, served with eight different clubs between 1946 and 1959: Sunderland, Spennymoor United, Chesterfield, Hull City, Nottingham Forest, Coventry City, Swindon Town and Rochdale.

In September 1946 when Swindon Town beat Exeter City 2-0 in a Third Division (South) game, the goals were scored by the Stephens twins, Alfred and William, the first time this had happened in League football.

The Morgan brothers, Roger and Ian, were the first twins to play together in the same team in the top flight of English football, doing so for QPR in 1968.

The Chambers twins, Adam and James, were the first to appear together in the English Premiership, for West Bromwich Albion against Arsenal at The Hawthorns on Boxing Day 2002.

Identical twins David and Peter Jackson were regulars in Bradford City's first team from 1954 to 1961 while two other sets of twins – Alan and Christopher Rhodes (1963/64) and Alan and Alex Smith (1967/68) – were also registered at Valley Parade at the same time.

Brothers David and Robert Thomas were a wonderful double act for Plymouth Argyle in 1946/47. They both played in 41 League games for the Pilgrims and scored 19 and 17 goals respectively.

The four MacLaren brothers of the 1950s were all goalkeepers – Jimmy with Chester and Carlisle United; Roy with Bury and Sheffield Wednesday; Dave with Leicester City and Plymouth Argyle and Monty with Liverpool.

Three Worthington brothers played every single Football League game for their respective clubs in the 1970/71 season: Frank (Huddersfield Town), Bob (Notts County) and David (Grimsby Town).

David and Neil Gregory became the first brothers to appear in the same starting line-up at a Wembley play-off final, doing so for Colchester United v. Torquay United in May 1998.

Between 1914 and 1929, eleven Keetley brothers from a Derby family played football, nine of them being professionals. They were Bill, Albert, John, Arthur, Joe, Tom, Frank, Harold and Charlie. The others were Lawrie and Sidney and there was also a sister. Tom and Frank Keetley are the only brothers to each score six goals in a League game.

Brothers James, John, Fred, Horace and Harold Wallbanks were all professionals with Football League clubs between 1929 and 1948.

During the 1922/23 season Clapton Orient had three sets of brothers on their books: James and Robert Duffus, John and Samuel Tonner and Owen and Thomas Williams.

The Scottish brothers Frank and Hugh O'Donnell played together in the same forward line for St Agatha's school (Leven, Fifeshire), Denbeath Violet, Wellesley Juniors, Celtic and Preston North End before the Second World War and for Blackpool, Heart of Midlothian and Liverpool during the hostilities.

The Charlton brothers, Jack (Middlesbrough) and Bobby (Preston North End), were the respective team managers of the two clubs mentioned when they opposed each other in a League game in 1974. Twenty-four years later, in 1998, the Little brothers, Alan (York City) and Brian (Stoke City) did likewise, also in a League game.

Family Affairs

Cousins Clive and Paul Allen played for Tottenham Hotspur against Coventry City in the 1987 FA Cup final. Paul's uncle Les Allen had been in Spurs' double-winning team of 1961 and in 1982 Clive also lined up for Queens Park Rangers against Spurs in that season's FA Cup final.

Three other members of the Allen family (above) played in the Football League. They were Les's son, Bradley (who made his debut for QPR), uncle Dennis (a player with Charlton Athletic, Reading and Bournemouth) and Martin (QPR, West Ham United, Portsmouth and Southend United).

By 1881, Notts County had had at least two members from eight different families: Greenhalgh, Cursham, Ashwell, Morse, Dobson, Shelton, Jessop and Oswald.

Every member of a football club (fifteen in all, twelve of whom were related) formed in Porthall, Donegal, Ireland in 1935, was named Crawford. For one of their matches, the referee and one of the linesmen were also named Crawford.

When Dave McCulloch, the former Brentford, Derby County and Leicester City Scottish international centre forward, signed for Third Lanark in 1932, he met his cousin, Tommy Waddell, for the first time in his life. Waddell had, a few minutes earlier, joined the same club.

In 2001/02, Rushden & Diamonds had two David Bells on their professional staff, one born in 1984, the other in 1985. They were cousins.

Scottish international Jimmy Blair, Cardiff City's star of the 1920s, had three children, all of whom were born in different countries – in Scotland, Wales and England.

Herbert Turner and Dai Astley were club-mates, internationals with the same country and brothers-in-law. They played together for Charlton Athletic and Wales prior to the Second World War – a Football League first.

Frank Blunstone of Chelsea came from a family of thirteen children. Jimmy Conway (Fulham) was one of twelve children, as was Tony Byrne (Southampton), while Jimmy Melia (Wolves, Liverpool and Brighton & Hove Albion) was one of eleven.

Father and Son

Plymouth Argyle manager Bob Jack sold three of his sons, David, Robert and Rollo, to Bolton Wanderers during the 1920s.

Jimmy Dunn (Everton) and Alec Herd (Manchester City) played against each in the 1933 FA Cup final. Later their sons Jimmy Dunn junior and David Herd won the trophy, Jimmy with Wolves in 1949 and David with Manchester United in 1963.

When Sheffield United won the FA Cup in 1902, one of their full-backs was Peter Boyle while playing at left half was Harry Johnson. In 1925, the Blades

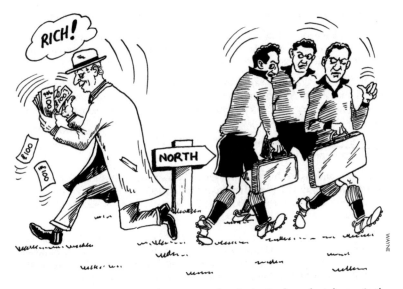

were FA Cup winners again and once more they had a Boyle and a Johnson in the line-up – Tommy at inside right and Harry at centre forward – the sons of those early United stars. The next time United reached the FA Cup final (in 1936 v. Arsenal) Tommy Johnson, the youngest son of old 'Harry' played at centre half, but he couldn't complete a hat-trick of wins as the Gunners took the trophy 1-0.

The Easthams, George senior and George junior, were the first father and son to play for England at senior level and also to become Football League managers. They played together for Ards in the Irish League in 1954/55.

Father Jack Butler and his son William appeared together in Grimsby Town's first team in 1916/17, while Alec Herd (father) and son (David) played in Stockport County's side as inside forwards v. Hartlepool United in 1950/51.

In the 1920s Jimmy Nelson and Jimmy Blair were renowned Scottish international full-back partners with Cardiff City. After the Second World War the respective sons of both players, Jimmy Blair junior (1947-1949) and Tony Nelson (1956-1964) were inside forwards with Bournemouth.

Jimmy Milne of Preston missed the 1938 FA Cup final through injury. His son, Gordon (Liverpool) then missed the 1965 final for the same reason.

Bill Dodgin and his son, also named Bill, both managed Fulham and Brentford.

There has been only one instance of a family trio filling the same position in international matches. Billy Scott, younger brother Elisha Scott and brother-in-law Bert Mehaffy all kept goal for Northern Ireland.

When Billy McCracken was manager of Hull City in the 1920s, he signed goalkeeper George Maddison. After the Second World War McCracken, who by now had taken over as boss of Aldershot, recruited Maddison's son, George junior, who was also a goalkeeper.

Father and son Ian and Gary Bowyer played together for Hereford United against Scunthorpe United in April 1990.

Fred Everiss and his son Alan Everiss were associated with West Bromwich Albion for a combined total of 121 years, Fred from 1896 to 1951 (as clerk, secretary-manager and director) and Alan from 1933 to 1999 (as clerk, assistant secretary, secretary, shareholder, director and life member).

Hubert Pearson kept goal for West Bromwich Albion in the 1912 FA Cup final; nineteen years later, in 1931, his son, Harold, was the Baggies' last line of defence against Birmingham, and likewise in 1935 against Sheffield Wednesday. Both father and son were together as registered players at The Hawthorns in 1925.

On the same day in April 1936, Harry Wait was Walsall's first-team goalkeeper while his son, Harold junior, was in goal for the Second XI.

Football Firsts

Football League

Aston Villa were the first club to reach the milestone of 6,000 League goals when Mark Walters scored against Bournemouth in a Second Division game in October 1987. Villa were also the first club to complete 100 League Cup matches, doing so in 1980/81.

Everton became the first club to compete in 3,000 First Division matches when they visited Brighton & Hove Albion on 7 October 1980.

Bradford Park Avenue and Oldham Athletic were the first clubs to meet each other in four different Divisions of the Football League: First, Second, Third and Fourth.

WAYNE

The first club to play in the Football League with 'City' as part of their name was Lincoln City, in the Second Division, in 1892.

The first League goal of the new millennium was scored by Brighton & Hove Albion's Darren Freeman after 100 seconds against Exeter City on 3 January 2000.

On 6 October 1965, Coventry City staged the first closed-circuit TV football match when a crowd of 10,200 watched their 2-1 Second Division win at Ninian Park, Cardiff on four large screens at their Highfield Road ground.

Colchester United were the first club to stage a commercially sponsored League game. In September 1973, their home game with Crewe Alexandra was sponsored by a local newspaper that provided money for pre-match entertainment.

Wolves were the first of the twelve founder members of the Football League to win the championship of the Third Division (North) (1924), the Second Division (1932), the First Division (1954), the Fourth Division (1988), the Third Division (1989), the FA Cup (1893) and the Football League Cup (1974). They also won the War Cup (1942), the Texaco Cup (1971), the Sherpa Van Trophy (1988) and the Division One play-off final (2003).

Wigan Borough were the first club to resign from the Football League during the course of a season, doing so in October 1931.

The first professional football match played on a Sunday in England was between Wisbech Town and Dunstable Town in the Southern League, on 19 March 1967.

The first team to win the Football League title after the First World War was West Bromwich Albion who did so in 1919/20 by gaining a record 28 wins, scoring a record 104 goals and securing a record 60 points. Their inside left Fred Morris also scored a club record 37 goals including five in an 8-0 victory over Notts County.

Wilf Milne scored the first League goal of his career in his 501st game for Swansea Town in 1934.

Sunderland were the first team to score 100 League goals in a season, doing so in 1892/93 (First Division).

Huddersfield Town were the first club that had won the League Championship to play in the Fourth Division.

The first penalty ever scored in a Football League game was by Joe Heath for Wolves against Accrington in September 1891.

The first black footballer to appear at competitive level may well have been Andrew Watson (born in of a West Indian mother in 1857) who served with Queen's Park (Glasgow), London Swifts, the Corinthians and Bootle. Capped by Scotland against England and Wales in 1881 and again against England in 1882, he won the Scottish Cup three times in the 1880s with Queen's Park.

Artificial Pitches

Stirling Albion were the first Scottish team to play on an artificial pitch, doing so in the 1967/68 season.

Queens Park Rangers were the first Football League club to install an artificial playing surface, doing so for the 1981/82 season.

Internationals

The first foreign/overseas-born player to win a full England cap was Bill Kenyon-Slaney (born in Rajkote, India in 1847) who made his debut in March 1873 against Scotland.

Jack Fort of Millwall became the first Third Division player to win a full England cap when he appeared against Belgium in May 1921.

Centre forward Joe Baker became the first player to represent England in a full international while on the books of a club outside the Football League. He was with Hibernian when he won his first cap against Northern Ireland in November 1959.

Billy Wright (Wolves) was the first player worldwide to win 100 international caps for one country, reaching that milestone when skippering England against Scotland at Wembley in April 1959.

European

The first Italian to win the coveted European Footballer of the Year award was Omar Sivori.

Birmingham City were the first English club to compete in a major European Cup competition, entering the Inter-Cities Fairs Cup in 1956.

Hibernian were the first British team to play in Europe, entering the European Cup in 1955/56.

To Wales

The first time a domestic trophy was taken out of England after the Second World War was in 1994 when Swansea City won the Autoglass Trophy. Cardiff City had been the first ever, winning the FA Cup in 1927.

Foreign Bodies

William Andrews was probably the first North American ever to play in the Football League, doing so for Grimsby Town in 1912/13. He was born in Kansas City and was capped for Ireland.

West Bromwich Albion were the first British professional club side to win a game in Russia, beating Dynamo Tbilisi 3-0 in June 1957. They also defeated the Russia Red Army side, CSKA Moscow, 4-2.

The UK's first Sikh football team (with all eleven players wearing turbans) participated in the Bloxwich Combination as Sikh Hunters in 1967/68.

Other Firsts

The first FWA Footballer of the Year, and indeed the first European Footballer of the Year, was Stanley Matthews, in 1948 and 1956 respectively. Matthews won the former award again in 1963. The first player to win the European award twice was Alfredo Di Stefano in 1957 and 1959.

FIFA's first World Footballer of the Year was Lothar Matthaus (Germany) in 1991. Brazil's Ronaldo was the first player to win the prize twice, in 1996 and 1997.

World Soccer's first World Player of the Year was the Italian Paolo Rossi in 1982. The Frenchman Michel Platini was the first player to receive the award twice, in 1984 and 1985.

On 23 December 2000, Motherwell's Steve Hammell became the first Scottish footballer to be charged with racially abusing a fellow professional, St Johnstone's Momo Sylla.

Macclesfield Town, now a Football League club, were the first winners of the FA Trophy, lifting the prize in May 1970 with a 2-0 win over Telford United.

Exeter City became the first English club to undertake an extensive tour of South America, doing so in the summer of 1914 when they played eight matches in Argentina and Brazil, losing only one.

The first player to be officially loaned out to another club in the Football League in the modern era was John Decker, who switched from Coventry City to Torquay United on a month's temporary transfer in July 1967.

In 14 September 1955, floodlights were used for the first time in FA Cup history at Aggborough for the preliminary round tie between Kidderminster Harriers and Brierley Hill Alliance. A crowd of 2,230 saw the Harriers win 4-2.

Carlisle United were the first Football League club outside London to install floodlights, doing so in 1952.

Everton were the first club to win the Second and First Division titles and the FA Cup in consecutive years, 1931-1933.

In 1927/28, Huddersfield Town became the first team to finish runners-up in both the Football League Championship and FA Cup in the same season.

Shin pads were first introduced in 1874 by Sam Weller Widdowson, the Nottingham Forest forward, who wore them strapped over his stockings.

When Mrs Lester became a director of Edinburgh Hibernian in 1927 she was the first woman to hold such a position within a first-class Association Football League club.

In October 1983 Tottenham Hotspur became the first British football club to sell their shares on the Stock Exchange.

On 11 November 2000, the PFA agreed to admit women for the first time in their ninety-three-year history by accepting fourteen full-time professionals of Fulham Ladies FC.

Football League

Teams

At the end of the 1907/08 season both Arsenal and Blackburn Rovers had identical playing records:

P	W	D	L	F	A	Pts
38	12	12	14	51	63	36

The clubs shared fourteenth position in the table.

Arsenal have been members of the top flight of English football since 1919 – a record for unbroken service.

Liverpool is the only city that has had a team in the top flight of English football every season since 1888.

Everton were the first team to complete 3,000 League games.

Rochdale went 28 League games without a win between November 1931 and September 1932.

League Goalscoring

Ted MacDougall was the first player to be top scorer in three different divisions of the Football League and his first 100 goals for Bournemouth (from 1968 onwards) came in only 122 matches.

In December 1927, centre forward Jimmy Cookson reached the milestone of 100 League goals in only his eighty-ninth match for West Bromwich Albion when he scored against South Shields in a Second Division fixture. Cookson also holds the record for scoring the most goals in a League game for the Baggies – six versus Blackpool, also in 1927.

Arthur Rowley (West Brom, Fulham, Leicester City and Shrewsbury Town) holds the record for scoring the most League goals in career, totalling 434 between 1947 and 1965.

League Snippets

Not one single corner kick was awarded during the League game between Newcastle United and Portsmouth in December 1931.

Bradford City and Chelsea were elected to the Football League in 1903 and 1905 respectively before they had played a competitive match of any kind.

Owing to the arctic winter, there was a break of only seventy days between the end of the 1946/47 League season and the start of the following campaign.

The Barrow v. Gillingham League game in October 1961 lasted only seventy-five minutes. In that time Barrow scored seven goals without reply before bad light stopped play. The result was allowed to stand.

Only Preston North End (22 games in 1888/89) and Arsenal (38 in 2003/04) have gone through a complete season of top-flight League football without losing a single match.

Arsenal equalled Nottingham Forest's forty-two-match unbeaten League run from 1977 and 1978 with a 5-3 home Premiership win over Middlesbrough on 22 August 2004. The Gunners then claimed a new record four days later with a 4-1 win at Norwich and went on to stretch the run to forty-nine games before losing away to Manchester United in October 2004.

Foreign Affairs

Celtic's Swedish international Henrik Larsson set a new record on 13 August 2003 when he scored his thirty-first goal in all European competitions against MTK of Hungary.

In 1973 the volcano on the Vestmann Islands off Iceland erupted violently and the local football club, IVB (FC Valur), had to flee their ground. Four years later, in September 1977, a new pitch was dug out and made fit to stage a UEFA Cup encounter with Glentoran in September 1979. A crowd of 5,800 attended to see the home side cause an upset by winning 1-0.

Preben Arentoft is the only player to have appeared for two different clubs in the same European competition in the same season. In the 1968/69 Fairs Cup, he starred for Morton against Chelsea in the first round and then for Newcastle United against Rangers and Ujpesti Dosza in the semi-final and final.

Leeds United played clubs from six different countries during their 1970/71 Fairs Cup exploits – the clubs came from Czechoslovakia, East Germany, England, Italy, Norway and Spain.

In the late 1970s and early 1980s, German international Ulu Stielike was on the losing side in a World Cup final, two European Cup finals and a European Cup-Winners'

Cup final. On a brighter note, however, he helped his country win the European Championships, clinched six League titles (three in Germany, three in Spain), gained one German and two Spanish Cup-winning medals and helped Real Madrid win the UEFA Cup in 1985.

On 15 August 1998, Chelsea started their Premiership game against Coventry City at Highfield Road with eleven full internationals in their line-up: three Italians, two Frenchmen, two Englishmen and one each from Holland, Nigeria, Spain and Uruguay. Two more, an Italian and a Norwegian, came on as substitutes... a record at that time.

Chelsea also created a new record on Boxing Day 1999 when manager Gianluca Vialli did not name an Englishman (indeed, not even a British player) in his starting line-up for the away Premiership game with Southampton. The team was: De Goey, Ferrer, Babayaro, Deschamps, Leboeuf, Emerson Thome, Petrescu, Di Matteo, Flo, Poyet, Ambrosetti. Jody Morris (born in Hammersmith, London) came on as a second-half substitute.

Allan Simonsen scored in the finals of all three major European club competitions in the space of seven years – for Borussia Mönchengladbach in the UEFA Cup of 1975 and European Cup of 1977 and for Barcelona in the Cup-Winners' Cup in 1982.

Real Madrid had four different managers between 1955 and 1960 during which time they won the European Cup on five occasions.

Spanish winger Francisco Gento (Real Madrid) scored in eleven consecutive European competitions (1955-1966). He netted 23 goals in all in 75 appearances – a record at that time. Gento played in eight European Cup finals and was a winner six times.

By 2005, full-back Gary Neville (Manchester United) had appeared in more European Champions League matches than any other player (over 80). Raul (Real Madrid) was close behind.

Swedish winger Kurt Hamrin scored in the European Cup-Winners' Cup finals of 1961 and 1962 (for Fiorentina) and 1968 (for AC Milan).

Going into the last fortnight of the 1966/67 season, Inter Milan were on course for the treble but in the end won nothing. They lost in the final of the European Cup to Celtic, finished runners-up in Serie A to Juventus by a point and crashed out of the Italian Cup in the semi-final, beaten by Serie B side Padua.

Carlos Rexach of Barcelona scored in two European Cup-Winners' Cup finals ten years apart: 1969 and 1979. The Spanish club lost the first but won the second.

The first British club to have twenty full internationals on their books were Manchester United in 1972/73: eight from Scotland, five from England, three from Northern Ireland, three from the Republic of Ireland and one from Wales.

Manchester United in fact had at least one player capped at senior level in each of the first twenty-five seasons following the Second World War.

Five international players scored for Third Division Burnley *v.* Scunthorpe United in December 1983. They were Martin Dobson, Kevin Reeves and Denis Tueart (England), Tommy Hutchison (Scotland) and Brian Flynn (Wales).

England did not field an unchanged team in their first thirty-six years of international football. Finally, in match number ninety-eight against Bohemia in Prague on 13 June 1908, the same XI that had beaten Hungary 7-0 in Budapest three days earlier went out and won 4-0. For the next game, however, nine changes were made.

Mickey Thomas was capped by Wales while with each of seven different Football League clubs: Wrexham, Manchester United, Everton, Brighton & Hove Albion, Stoke City, Chelsea and West Bromwich Albion. Irishman Joe Harvey won caps with six different clubs while centre half Dave Watson won England recognition with five.

Goalkeepers

League Football

Brothers Alan and Gary Kelly lined up as opposing goalkeepers for Preston North End and Bury respectively in a League game on 13 January 1990. Their father Alan senior had previously kept goal for Preston.

Harry Morton was seated in the stand at Maine Road ready to watch Manchester City play Aston Villa in a First Division game in November 1930. Five minutes before kick-off he was summoned to the dressing room and asked to make his League debut for Villa when regular goalkeeper Fred Biddlestone was injured warming-up.

David Herd (Manchester United) scored against three different Sunderland goalkeepers in the same League game in November 1966: Jim Montgomery, Charlie Hurley and John Parke.

Luton Town are the only club, certainly since the Second World War, to have chosen two goalkeepers to play at centre forward in League games. They did it with Ron Baynham against Leyton Orient on Easter Monday 1962 and with Tony Read in several games during the 1960s.

In 1964/65, goalkeeper Ken Mulhearn was registered with Stockport County who finished ninety-second and last in the Football League. Three years later he was a member of Manchester City's First Division Championship-winning team.

In 1933, Alex Mackay, born 30 August 1913, was signed by Southport, his sixth League club. When he made his debut for Southport, he had tasted League football in all four divisions and still hadn't reached the age of twenty. His other clubs had been Wolves, Hull City, Newcastle United, Bolton Wanderers and Bournemouth.

Goalkeeper John Hope appeared in all four divisions of the Football League in the course of seven appearances covering five seasons. He lined up for Darlington (Third and Fourth Divisions) in 1966/67 and 1967/68, for Newcastle United (First Division) in 1968/69 and Sheffield United (Second Division) in 1970/71.

Reading goalkeeper Arthur Wilkie scored twice in a 4-2 League win over Halifax Town match in August 1962 after moving to the wing with a hand injury.

In January/February 1928, Rochdale were forced to field five different goalkeepers in a run of six games.

WAYNE

Goalkeeper Fred Craig scored five penalties for Plymouth Argyle in 362 League games during the 1920s.

On 27 December 1994, nineteen-year-old goalkeeper Paul Pettinger was chauffeur-driven 300 miles in a Rolls-Royce from Leeds to Torquay United's Plainmoor ground to make his debut against Hartlepool United. The game ended 2-2.

Steve Milton let in thirteen goals on his League debut for Halifax Town against Stockport County in January 1934, while Billy O'Rourke conceded seven goals when making his League bow for Burnley against QPR in October 1970.

Aberdeen 'keeper Bobby Clark went 1,156 minutes (almost thirteen matches) without conceding a goal during the 1970/71 season. Graeme Crawford of York City went eleven games without giving away a goal in 1973/74.

Goalkeeper John Croates made his League debut in 1966/67 for Chester. His second game followed ten years later for Southport.

On 25 April 1936, Blackburn Rovers used five different goalkeepers in only eight First Division games covering forty-three days. They were Binns (the fifth to be chosen), Hughes, Barron, Hamill and Pratt.

Bob Anderson helped Bristol City win the Third Division (South) Championship in 1955 and three years later was in the Bristol Rovers side that won the same title.

Goalkeeper Marc De Clerck scored on his debut for Aberdeen against Berwick Rangers in August 1980.

The League appearance record for a goalkeeper in Scottish football is held by Jim Gallacher who, in 1992 at the age of forty, appeared in his 642nd game of his career for Clydebank. Peter Shilton, with 1,005, holds the record for the most Football League appearances.

In 1995/96, when Gillingham conceded only 20 goals in 46 League games, their 'keeper Jim Stannard kept 29 clean sheets to equal the all-time record of shut-outs in one campaign. The record for clean sheets in a League career (for one club) is seventy-one, achieved by Bradford City's Paul Tomlinson between 1987 and 1994.

Chris Woods didn't let a goal in for 1,196 minutes playing for Rangers between 26 November 1986 and 31 January 1987.

Steve Death of Reading holds the record for the Football League, not conceding a goal for 1,103 minutes between 24 March and 18 August 1979.

Petr Cech (Chelsea) did not concede a goal in 1,025 minutes of Premiership football between December 2004 and March 2005. And at 2009 David James (Portsmouth) had kept a record number of clean sheets in the Premiership (150+).

Cup Action

Fred Mitchell is the only goalkeeper on record to have played in an FA Cup final wearing spectacles, doing so for Preston North End against Huddersfield Town in 1922.

Dick Pym played in three FA Cup winning teams with Bolton Wanderers (1923, 1926 and 1929) and never conceded a goal.

Three different players kept goal for Leicester Fosse in an 8-2 League defeat at Leeds United in October 1938.

The Foxes again used three different 'keepers during their League game v. Wolves in March 1976 (which they drew 2-2) and likewise in a home FA Cup tie with Shrewsbury Town in March 1982 (which they won 5-2).

Chris Woods was the first goalkeeper to appear in a Wembley final before making his Football League debut, doing so for Nottingham Forest against Liverpool in the League Cup of March 1978.

John Gilfillan kept goal for East Fife in the Scottish Cup final of 1927 and for Portsmouth when they competed in the 1929 and 1934 FA Cup finals. He was a loser each time.

Manchester City's German goalkeeper Bert Trautmann broke his neck in the 1956 FA Cup final against Birmingham City. A year later Manchester United's 'keeper Ray Wood did likewise against Aston Villa.

Two goalkeepers who were injured – Terry Adlington for Torquay United (v. Barnet) and Mike Grainger for Halifax Town (v. Workington) – scored in FA Cup ties on 16 November 1963.

European/Overseas

Atletico Madrid's thirty-one-year-old goalkeeper Abel Resino holds the world record for playing the longest time without conceding a goal. During the years 1990 and 1991 he had a goal-less run of 1,275 minutes in Spanish football.

Spanish heart-throb singer Julio Iglesias was once registered as a goalkeeper with Real Madrid.

International Number Ones

Four goalkeepers were used in the England v. Wales international at Wrexham in March 1908. Horace Bailey (England) and Leigh Richmond Roose (Wales) started the game but Roose was injured and subsequently replaced by full-back Charlie Morris (Derby County). In the second half David Davies (Bolton Wanderers) came on as a substitute, allowing Morris to move back into his outfield position.

Wolves provided both goalkeepers for the Victory International at The Hawthorns in 1945: Bert Williams (England) and Cyril Sidlow (Wales).

Frank Haffey was the Scottish goalkeeper when England beat their arch rivals 9-3 in an international match at Wembley in 1963.

Goalkeeper Neville Southall (Wales), Pat Jennings (Northern Ireland) and Peter Shilton (England) all hold the record for gaining the most international caps for their respective countries.

Two of the smallest goalkeepers ever to play for England at senior level were Alan Hodgkinson (Sheffield United) and Teddy Davison (Sheffield Wednesday). Both were 5ft 7in tall. Davison was manager at Bramall Lane in 1953 when he signed Hodgkinson on professional forms.

In 1954 England selected Doncaster Rovers goalkeeper Ken Hardwick for an Under-23 international trial – and then found out he was aged thirty!

In 1958/59 Scotland chose Hearts goalkeeper Gordon Marshall for their international squad before finding out he was an Englishman, born in Farnham.

Hugh Kelly had a nightmare international debut for Northern Ireland in November 1949, conceding nine goals against England at Maine Road.

Keeping Up Appearances

Until 1912 a goalkeeper was allowed to use his hands anywhere on the field of play.

There were five professional goalkeepers registered with Sheffield Wednesday in season 1957/58 but manager Eric Taylor preferred an amateur, Mike Pinner, most of the time.

Crystal Palace goalkeeper John Jackson did not miss a single League or cup game for five seasons, 1967/68-1971/72. He had one run of 222 consecutive League appearances for the Eagles and later played in 210 consecutive matches for Leyton Orient.

Bill 'Fatty' Foulke weighed over twenty-five stone at one stage during a career that spanned thirteen years from 1894 to 1907.

Joe Reader of West Bromwich Albion was the last goalkeeper to discard long white trousers. He was also the only player to appear in competitive games for Albion on three different home grounds: Four Acres, Stoney Lane and The Hawthorns.

On the same day in April 1936, Harry Wait was Walsall's first-team goalkeeper against Barrow, while his son, Harry junior, kept goal for the Saddlers' reserve side.

Goalkeeper Willie Robb played for Birmingham against Bristol City on 24 April 1915; his next League outing followed seventeen years later when he lined up for Aldershot against Southend United on 27 August 1932. In between times he played in Scotland with Rangers and Hibernian.

During the 1971/72 season Hartlepool United fielded a different goalkeeper in four successive League games: Mick Gadsby, Barry Noble, Eddie Nalshett and Ron Hillyard.

Peter Grotier played in four different West Ham United teams in the space of eight days in April 1969.

Birmingham and England goalkeeper Harry Hibbs was the only player to receive a benefit during the Second World War (v. Aston Villa in April 1940).

The respective goalkeepers in the 1969 FA Cup final had both scored League goals: Manchester City's Harry Dowd had obliged for Bury in February 1964 and Leicester's Peter Shilton for the Foxes against Southampton in October 1967.

The German Bert Trautmann was the first goalkeeper to be named Footballer of the Year in England, collecting the award in 1956 after gaining an FA Cup winners' medal.

After Scottish goalkeeper Ian McKechnie had been given a free transfer by Southend United in May 1966 he wrote to twenty other clubs asking for a job. Only one replied, Hull City, for whom he went on to appear in 255 League and cup games.

Walsall used seven different goalkeepers during the 1972/73 season: Wesson, Peacock, John Osborne (an FA Cup winner with WBA in 1968), Johnson, Turner, Ball and Inger.

A late, late goal by Carlisle United goalkeeper Jimmy Glass earned the Cumbrian side a 2-2 draw in the final League game of the 1998/99 season at home to Plymouth Argyle. The point gained kept United in the Football League. Scarborough dropped into the Conference instead.

On 15 March 1902, Blackpool's regular goalkeeper Jack Dorrington missed the team's train at Preston en route for a Second Division match at Leicester. The club's secretary Tom Barcroft took over between the posts in a 1-0 defeat.

League Football

When Leeds United beat Chelsea 7-0 in a League game at Elland Road in October 1967, all the goals were scored by different players. This was the first time this had happened in a competitive match.

Manchester City are the only team to date to have scored 100 goals (100 exactly) and conceded 100 goals (104) in the same season, 1957/58, when they finished fifth in the First Division.

On the first day of the offside law, 29 August 1925, Aston Villa beat Burnley 10-0.

In January 1975 nine different players figured on the scoresheet when Plymouth Argyle beat Bournemouth 7-3 at Dean Court. The only player to score twice was Paul Mariner for the Pilgrims.

Jack Doran scored all of Brighton & Hove Albion's first fifteen Third Division (South) goals at the start of the 1921/22 season. He finished up with a total of twenty-three. Doran earned the DCM and MM during the First World War.

In season 1962/63 Crystal Palace had nine players on their books whose combined tally of goals was in excess of 1,000.

Bolton Wanderers scored in twenty-four consecutive League games covering two campaigns, 1888/89 and 1889/90 (twenty-two in one season, two in the next), and again in the 1996/97 season.

David Thomas of Plymouth Argyle and Ralph Hunt and Ron Rafferty of Grimsby Town each scored in ten successive League games in the 1946/47, 1959/60 and 1961/62 seasons respectively.

Aston Villa conceded seven goals at home three times in 1935/36, losing 7-0 to West Bromwich Albion, 7-1 to Arsenal and 7-2 to Middlesbrough. They also lost 6-2 to Grimsby Town. In all Villa gave away a total of 110 goals in their 42 First Division games that season, suffering relegation in the process.

The last time two players from the same team each scored thirty or more League goals in the same season was in 1935/36 when the Sunderland duo of Raich Carter and Bob Gurney obliged with 31 apiece.

Luckless Merthyr Town conceded 135 League goals during their 1929/30 Third Division (South) campaign.

Four players, namely Lol Chappell for Barnsley at Bristol City in 1958; Ron Rafferty for Grimsby Town at Lincoln City, also in 1958; Tony Hateley for Aston Villa at Tottenham in 1966; and Kerry Dixon for Reading at Doncaster Rovers in 1982, have scored four goals in an away League game yet failed to finish on the winning side.

The following players all scored five goals in away Football League games: Jimmy McIntosh for Blackpool at Preston in 1948; Jimmy Greaves for Chelsea, also at Preston in 1959; Bobby Tambling for Chelsea against Aston Villa in 1966; Tony Woodcock for Arsenal also against Aston Villa in 1983; and Gordon Durie for Chelsea at Walsall in 1989.

Gillingham's Damien Richardson scored his first and 100th League goals against the same club, Mansfield Town, in November 1972 and March 1980 respectively.

Gary Taylor-Fletcher (for Huddersfield Town v. Scunthorpe) scored the 500,000th goal in the Football League in August 2006.

Blackburn had six goals disallowed when beating Liverpool 1–0 in September 1896.

Torquay United failed to score in 13 of 21 League games between November 1990 and March 1991.

In 2006–07 Stockport created a new record by winning nine successive League games without conceding a goal.

West Bromwich Albion's Tony Brown scored his first League goal past the Ipswich Town 'keeper Roy Bailey in 1963. Fifteen years later Brown scored his 213th goal for the Baggies past Roy's son Gary, who was then keeping goal for Manchester United.

Jimmy Greaves is the youngest player (at twenty years 261 days) to reach the milestone of 100 goals, doing so for Chelsea in 1960. Greaves has also scored more goals in the English First Division than any other player: 357 in total comprising 124 for Chelsea, 220 for Tottenham and 13 for West Ham United. He scored against thirty-six of the thirty-eight clubs he opposed, missing out against Huddersfield and Crystal Palace.

Wilf Milne failed to score a goal in his first 500 League appearances for Swansea Town up to April 1934, but in his 501st he found the net against Lincoln City.

Newport County are the only club to have conceded eleven goals in a League match twice since the Second World War. They lost 13-0 at Newcastle United in October 1946 and 11-1 at Notts County in January 1949.

Wolves scored over 100 League goals four seasons running from 1957/58 to 1960/61, weighing in with 103, 110, 106 and 103 respectively for a total of 422 in 168 games.

Peterborough United scored 334 in their first three seasons of League football, 1961/62-1963/64, totalling 134, 107 and 93. Aston Villa netted 304 in three seasons of First Division football from 1930/31 to 1932/33 including 190 at home. In fact, Villa averaged over three goals a game in the 1930/31 season, scoring 86 in their 21 home League matches and 42 away for an overall total of 128 in 42 starts.

In the space of five seasons, 1956/57-1960/61, the 210 League games played by Charlton Athletic produced a total of 903 goals – 448 were scored by the Addicks and 457 by their opponents. Fans certainly got value for money with an average of 4.30 goals per game.

On 28 September 2002, Arsenal set an overall League record by scoring in their forty-seventh consecutive match, surpassing the record set by Chesterfield in 1930. They increased their goalscoring run to fifty-five games before failing to find the net against Manchester United at Old Trafford on 7 December 2002.

Alf Lythgoe scored five goals for Stockport County in each of the club's two Third Division games against Southport in August 1934. He then repeated this feat in the First Division the following April for Huddersfield Town against Blackburn Rovers.

Six goals were disallowed for offside during the Swindon Town v. Southend United Third Division (South) game in 1949.

Four goals were scored in just four minutes forty-four seconds of the Southampton v. Spurs Premiership game at The Dell in April 1995. Saints won 4-3. With half an hour remaining of the League game between Leeds United and Liverpool at Elland Road in April 1991, the Merseysiders were leading 4-0. The final score was Leeds 4 Liverpool 5.

Aston Villa were 4-0 down in their League game at Accrington in March 1893 but stormed back to win 6-4.

Leyton Orient led Watford 4-1 in a Southern League game in March 1904; the game finished Orient 4 Watford 7.

In a German League game in October 1973, Bayern Munich hit back to beat FC Kaiserslautern 7-4, having trailed 4-1 after fifty-seven minutes.

Eintracht Frankfurt trailed Vfb Stuttgart 3-0 after sixty-six minutes of a League game in August 1973. They fought back to win 4-3.

Also in Germany, in September 1976, Vfl Bochum were leading Bayern Munich 4-0 after fifty-three minutes. They eventually lost the game 6-5.

ree League goals in 1953/54 were scored for different clubs
Southend United (Third), Cardiff City (First) and Brentford

red six goals in twenty-nine minutes of their Second Division
ddersfield Town in December 1957, turning a 5-1 deficit into
ly ten men.

scored 20 or more goals in 1964/65: Gary Talbot (28), Mike
orris (24) and Hugh Ryden (20). The team scored 119 in total.

anchester City scored more goals (80) than any other team in
were still relegated.

scored 87 home League goals in the Third Division (South).

goals in 5 successive home League games in October and
ney beat Sheffield Wednesday 9-3, Newcastle United 8-3,
er City 9-2 and Middlesbrough 5-1. Dixie Dean claimed 17 of
goal hauls against Wednesday and Chelsea.

ol scored 8 goals over the course of 2 successive League games
single point. They lost 4-3 to Sheffield Wednesday and 6-5 to

gham conceded only 20 goals in 46 League games – a
Goalkeeper Jim Stannard kept 29 clean sheets, to equal the
ut-outs in one campaign.

Cup Action

, York City beat Burton Town 3-2 away in a first round FA Cup
George Bowater scoring one of the goals. A year later Burton
e same stage of the competition and this time Bowater scored

ored nine of Bournemouth's eleven goals against Margate in an
. 'Super Mac' netted seventeen FA Cup goals for the Cherries in
70 and 1971).

ored a record fifteen FA Cup goals for Southern League side
r in season 1900/01, including all four in a semi-final win over
bion.

Watford lost the first leg of a League Cup tie 4-0 at Southampton in 1980/81 but won the return fixture at Vicarage Road 7-1 to go through 7-5 on aggregate.

Sammy Armes, the Chester outside right, is the only player to have scored a total of nine goals in three consecutive matches from the extreme wing position. He netted four times against Rochdale and twice against Accrington Stanley before grabbing a hat-trick against Darlington in three Third Division (North) games during November and December 1933.

In 1937/38 five Arsenal players, Cliff Bastin, Ray Bowden, Ted Drake, Joe Hulme, and George Hunt, each had more than 100 League goals to his credit.

Kevin Bremner scored against Reading for three different clubs in 1982/83: Wrexham, Plymouth Argyle and Millwall. He also played and scored for Birmingham City and Colchester United in that same season, appearing in a total of forty-five League games.

The first three occasions that Everton scored six goals in an away League games were all at Derby – in 1890 (when they won 6-2), 1892 (6-1) and 1954 (6-2).

Eleven of Stockport County's goals in their record 13-0 home League win over Halifax Town in January 1934 were scored in the second half, between the fiftieth and eighty-eighth minutes, eight coming in one sixteen-minute spell.

Sunderland scored eight goals in twenty-eight minutes, the last five in eight, when they beat arch-rivals Newcastle United 9-1 away in December 1908.

West Bromwich Albion scored 18 goals in 3 League visits to Birmingham City – winning 5-3, 6-0 and 7-1 – between December 1957 and April 1960.

Nottingham Forest conceded 17 goals in their last 3 League games of 1909/10, losing 7-3, 6-0 and 4-0.

Spurs' Alan Gilzean failed to score in any of his club's 28 away League games between February 1965 and October 1966. He did, however, score 26 times at home.

The lowest total of goals scored by the leading marksman of a League Championship-winning side is 10 by Sunderland's Willie Hogg in season 1901/02.

Exeter City scored only 4 goals in their 21 away Third Division games in 1923/24 – the lowest tally in any division since the First World War.

Tom Phillipson of Wolves holds the record for scoring in consecutive League games – fifteen between November 1926 and February 1927. He netted a total of 22 goals.

Bill Prendegast scored in twelve consecutive Third Division (North) games and one FA Cup tie for Chester between September and December 1938.

The Scottish record holder is the Dane Finn Dossing, who scored in fifteen consecutive First Division matches for Dundee United in 1964/65.

In January 1984, Bristol City held a ballot among their supporters in order to decide whether Howard Pritchard or Alan Crawford should be credited with a League goal against Wrexham. Crawford got the vote.

Referee Mr Charles Sutcliffe disallowed seven goals in succession during the League game between Blackburn Rovers and Liverpool at Ewood Park in 1898/99.

In December 1954 two Leicester City players, Jack Froggatt and Stan Milburn, were credited with a 'shared' own goal. They struck the ball simultaneously past their keeper Johnny Anderson in a 3-1 League defeat by Chelsea.

In December 1958, two Hearts players, Willie Bauld and Jimmy Murray, were also credited with a 'shared' goal after heading the ball into the net against Aberdeen at Tynecastle. Both jumped and nodded Bobby Kirk's free-kick into the net together.

Grenville Morris (1902/03) and David 'Boy' Martin (1936/37) share the record for scoring in eight consecutive League games for Nottingham Forest.

Notts County scored a record total of 33 goals in 5 consecutive home League games against Newport County between 1948 and 1961, winning 11-1, 7-0, 6-0 and 8-1 and drawing 1-1.

Derek Stokes of Bradford City scored 25 goals in 15 games in 1959/60, Bobby Tambling of Chelsea netted 23 in 12 in 1962/63 and Geoff Hurst weighed in with 22 in 13 for West Ham United in 1966/67.

Centre half Dave Watson scored his first League goal for Notts County in 1967. His second came eighteen years later for the same club.

Newcastle United put 16 goals past the two Merseyside clubs in the space of a week in 1933, beating Everton 7-3 at Goodison Park on Boxing Day and hammering Liverpool 9-2 at St James' Park on New Year's Day. This was to no avail though as the Geordies were still relegated to the Second Division at the end of the season.

Lol Chappell scored four goals for Barnsley at Bristol City in August 1958 but still finished on the losing side as the Ashton Gate club won 7-4.

On Boxing Day 1935, the Third Division (North) game between Tranmere Rovers and Oldham Athletic produced seventeen goals, Rovers winning 13-4. In their next game Oldham beat Mansfield Town 4-1 while Rovers beat New Brighton 3-1.

Teddy Sheringham scored the 300th goal of his career and his 100th for Tottenham Hotspur in the same game, against Sunderland on 8 February 2003.

The Rowley brothers, Arthur and Jack [...] goals on the same day, 22 October [...] Manchester United.

The most goals scored by an out-and-[...] League and cup football is 33 by out[...] He also scored four in a home friendly [...] 21 the previous season.

The player who has scored the fastest [...] reached the target in eight years from 1[...]

Derek Dougan was the first Irishman to [...]

On 10 September 1932 Halifax Town [...] minutes remaining of a Third Division (N[...] Halifax 2 Wrexham 5 – the most strikin[...] Football League history.

Blackpool let in 125 goals in 1930/31, [...] relegation. Ipswich Town conceded 12[...] went down.

Frank Dudley's first [...] in different division[...] (Second).

Charlton Athletic sc[...] home game with H[...] a 7-6 victory with o[...]

Four Chester player[...] Metcalf (27), Elfed [...]

In season 1937/38 [...] the First Division b[...]

In 1927/28, Millwa[...]

Everton scored 38 [...] November 1931. [...] Chelsea 7-2, Leices[...] them including five[...]

In 1932/33 Blackp[...] and failed to earn [...] Blackburn Rovers.

In 1995/96, Gilli[...] competition recor[...] all-time record of [...]

In November 193[...] tie, York left wing[...] beat York 5-1 at t[...] for Burton.

Ted MacDougall s[...] FA Cup tie in 197[...] just over a year (1[...]

'Sandy' Brown sc[...] Tottenham Hotspur[...] West Bromwich A[...]

On 17 January 1891, a total of twenty-two goals were scored in two FA Cup ties played in the same city: Sheffield United lost 9-1 to Notts County while Wednesday beat Halliwell 12-0.

Wilf Minter scored seven goals for St Albans against Dulwich Hamlet in a replayed FA Cup tie in 1922 yet still finished on the losing side as Dulwich won 8-7.

Denis Law scored all of Manchester City's goals against Luton Town in a fourth-round FA Cup tie in January 1961 only for the game to be abandoned with City leading 6-2. Law scored again in the replay, which City lost 3-1.

Chelsea's Peter Osgood was the first player to score in the final of the FA Cup (1970), the European Cup-Winners' Cup (1971) and the League Cup (1972).

Stan Mortensen scored in twelve consecutive FA Cup games for Blackpool from 1945/46 to 1948/49 inclusive. This feat was equalled by Billy McAdams of Manchester City in 1957/58.

Jeff Astle of West Bromwich Albion was the first player to score in both the FA Cup and League Cup finals at Wembley, doing so against Everton and Manchester City in 1968 and 1970 respectively.

Crewe Alexandra conceded 18 goals in 2 fourth-round FA Cup games at White Hart Lane in successive seasons, losing 13-2 and 5-1 to Spurs in 1959/60 and 1960/61 respectively.

Henry Cursham scored a record 48 FA Cup goals for Notts County between 1880 and 1887.

Jim Fryatt's first four FA Cup goals were scored for as many clubs over a period covering nine seasons: Southend United (1960/61), Bradford Park Avenue (1964/65), Southport (1966/67) and Blackburn Rovers (1968/69).

The only player to take five-goal hauls in successive FA Cup ties is Harold Brooks for Aldershot in 1947 against Reading (won 7-3) and then Newport Isle of Wight (won 7-0).

International Scene

Vivian Woodward and Harold Bache both had the pleasure of scoring seven goals in a game for England in amateur international matches against France in 1906 and 1910 respectively. Willie Jordan scored six, also against France, in 1907.

High Scoring Games

Listed among the big scorelines in world football (with the winning team securing twelve or more goals) are the following:

Football League

Newcastle United 13-0 Newport County	1946
Stockport County 13-0 Halifax Town	1934
Tranmere Rovers 13-4 Oldham Athletic	1935*
Arsenal 12-0 Loughborough Town	1900
Chester 12-0 York City	1936
Darwen 12-0 Walsall	1896
Leicester Fosse 12-0 Nottingham Forest	1909
Luton Town 12-0 Bristol Rovers	1936
Small Heath 12-0 Walsall Town Swifts	1892
Small Heath 12-0 Doncaster Rovers	1903
West Bromwich Albion 12-0 Darwen	1892
Barrow 12-1 Gateshead	1934
Aston Villa 12-2 Accrington	1892

* Most goals (17) ever scored in one League game

FA Cup

Preston North End 26-0 Hyde	1887
Preston North End 18-0 Reading	1894
Stocksbridge Park Steels 17-1 Oldham Town	2002
Wanderers 16-0 Farningham	1874
Southend United 16-1 Brentwood	1968
Notts County 15-0 Rotherham Town	1885
Royal Engineers 15-0 High Wycombe	1875
Darwen 15-0 Romford	1880
Clapton 0-14 Nottingham Forest	1891

Wolves 14-0 Crosswell's Brewery	1886
Aston Villa 13-0 Wednesbury Old Athletic	1886
Bolton Wanderers 13-0 Sheffield United	1890
Darwen 13-0 Kidderminster Harriers	1891
Leicester Fosse 13–0 Notts Olympic	1894
Aston Villa 13-1 Casuals	1890
Tottenham Hotspur 13-2 Crewe Alexandra	1960
Cheltenham Town 12-0 Chippenham	1935
Clapham Rovers 12-0 Leyton	1875
Bury 12-1 Stockton	1897
The Wednesday (Sheffield) 12-0 Halliwell	1891
Yeovil Town 12-1 Westbury United	1923
The Wednesday (Sheffield) 12-2 Spilsby	1882

Scottish League

Airdrieonians 15-1 Dundee Wanderers	1894
East Fife 13-2 Edinburgh City	1937
Dundee United 12-1 East Stirlingshire	1936
Motherwell 12-1 Dundee United	1954
King's Park 12-2 Forfar Athletic	1930

Scottish Cup

Arbroath 36-0 Bon Accord	1885
Dundee Harp 35-0 Aberdeen Rovers	1885
Stirling Albion 20-0 Selkirk	1984
Partick Thistle 16-0 Glasgow United	1960
Partick Thistle 16-0 Royal Albert	1931
Queen's Park 16-0 Royal Albert	1930
Queen's Park 16-0 St Peter's	1885
Hearts 15-0 Jamestown	1878

Hibernian 15-0 St Peter's	1885
Queen's Park 15-0 Shotts	1881
St Mirren 15-0 Glasgow University	1960
St Mirren 15-0 King's Park	1936
Queen's Park 15-1 Hurlford	1879
Vale of Leven 15-1 Peebles Rovers	1960
Dundee United 14-0 Nithsdale	1931
Forfar Athletic 14-1 Lindertis	1988
Hearts 14-1 Elgin City	1939
Rangers 14-2 Blairgowrie	1934
Aberdeen 13-0 Parkhead	1923
Dumbarton 13-1 Kirkintilloch Central	1888
Albion Rovers 12-0 Airdriehall	1897
Cowdenbeath 12-0 Johnstone	1928
Montrose 12-0 Vale of Lethen	1975
Brechin City 12-1 Thornhill	1926
Falkirk 12-1 Laurieston	1893

Other Scottish Cups

Hibernian 22-1 The 42nd Highlanders	1881
Hearts 21-0 Anchor	1880
Gretna 20-0 Silloth	1962
Elgin City 18-1 Brora Rangers	1960
Kilmarnock 15-0 Lanemark	1890

Highland League

Peterhead 17-0 Fort William	1998

European Competitions

Sporting Lisbon 16-1 Apoel Nicosia	ECWC, 1963
Ajax 14-0 Red Boys	UEFA Cup, 1984

Chelsea 13-0 Jeunesse Hautcharage	ECWC, 1971
Derby County 12-0 Finn Harps	UEFA Cup, 1976
Swansea City 12-0 Sliema Wanderers	ECWC, 1982
Feyenoord 12-2 KR Reykjavik	European Cup, 1969

Internationals (friendly and competitive)

Australia 31-0 American Samoa	2001
Libya 21-0 Oman	1966
England 20-0 France	Amateur, 1910
Iran 19-0 Guam	2000
Denmark 17-1 France 'A'	Olympics, 1908
English FA XI 17-0 Australia	Test match, 1951
Iran 17-0 Maldives	in Syria, 1997
Germany 16-0 USSR	Olympics, 1912
France 0-15 England	Amateur, 1906
Brazil 14-0 Nicaragua	1975
Denmark 14-2 Iceland	1967
Ireland 0-13 England	1882
Spain 13-0 Bulgaria	1933
San Marino 0–13 Germany	2006
Argentina 12-0 Ecuador	1942
Denmark 12-0 Norway	1917
Germany 12-0 Cyprus	1969
Hungary 12-0 Albania	1950
Hungary 12-0 Russia	1927
Latvia 0-12 Switzerland	1927
New Zealand 0-12 England FA	1937
England 12-1 Sweden	Olympics, 1948
New Zealand 1-12 England FA	1937
Spain 12-1 Malta	1983
England 12-2 Holland	Amateur, 1907

Others

Stoke 26-0 Mow	Staffordshire County Cup, 1877
West Bromwich Albion 26-0 Coseley	Birmingham Cup, 1882
Arsenal 26-1 Paris XI	Friendly, 1904
West Bromwich Albion 23-0 Burton Wanderers	Staffordshire Cup, 1889
Studley & District 2-23 West Bromwich Albion	Friendly, 1888
Asby 19-0 Krona	Swedish Int. League, 1966
Norwich City 18-0 Brighton	Wartime regional league, 1940
Stoke 16-0 Blackburn Rovers	Wartime Lancashire section, 1917
West Bromwich Albion 15-0 Bloxwich Strollers	Birmingham Cup, 1884
Alberta All Stars 0-15 West Bromwich Albion	Friendly, 1959
Krylbo IF 0-15 Norwich City	Friendly, 1993
Weiner Athletic Klub 14-0 Vienna CFC	Austrian League, 1912
SC Wacker 14-0 Kapfenberg	Austrian League, 1956

Goal Aces

Most goals scored in one match by one player

13   Archie Thompson (Australia) *v.* American Samoa, 2001
      John Petrie (Arbroath) *v.* Bon Accord, Scottish Cup, 1885
11   Stan Fazackerley (Hull City) *v.* Trondheim & District, Tour, 1912.
10   Gerry Baker (St Mirren) *v.* Glasgow University, Scottish Cup, 1960
      Joe Payne (Luton Town) *v.* Bristol Rovers, League, 1935
      Sofus Nielsen (Denmark) *v.* France, Olympic Games, London, 1908
      Gotfried Fuchs (Germany) *v.* Russia, Olympic Games, Stockholm, 1912
      Paul Jackson (Stocksbridge Park Steels) *v.* Oldham Town, FA Cup, 2002
      Joe Baker (Hibernian) *v.* Peebles Rovers, Scottish Cup, 1961
9   James Fleming (Rangers) *v.* Blairgowrie, Scottish Cup, 1934
      'Bunny' Bell (Tranmere Rovers) *v.* Oldham Athletic, League, 1935
      Ted MacDougall (Bournemouth) *v.* Margate, FA Cup, 1971
      Jock Simpson (Partick Thistle) *v.* Royal Albert, Scottish Cup, 1931
      Jim Hogg (Hartlepool United) *v.* Workington, NE League, 1910

8   Jimmy McGrory (Celtic) v. Dunfermline Athletic, League, 1928

Owen McNally (Arthurlie) v. Armadale, Scottish League, 1927

Jim Dyet (King's Park) v. Forfar Athletic, League, 1930+

John Calder (Morton) v. Raith Rovers, League, 1936

Jock Hayward (Raith Rovers) v. Brechin City, League, 1937

Davie Weir (Halliwell) v. Notts County, FA Cup, 1887

Billy Walsh (Hearts) v. King's Park, Scottish Cup, 1937

7   Karim Bagheri (Iran) v. Maldives, International, 1997

Tommy Briggs (Blackburn Rovers) v. Bristol Rovers, League, 1955

Albert Brown (Southampton) v. Northampton Town, Southern League, 1901

Gary Cole (Australia) v Fiji, International, 1981

Ted Drake (Arsenal) v. Aston Villa, League, 1935

Eric Gemmell (Oldham Athletic) v. Chester, League, 1952

Alan Gilzean (Dundee) v. Queen of the South, League, 1962

Tim Coleman (Stoke City) v. Lincoln City, League, 1957

Ted Hartson (Mansfield Town) v. Hartlepool United, League, 1937

Albert Juliussen (Dundee) v. Dunfermline Athletic, League, 1947

Koslicek II (SC Wacker) v. Kapfenberg, Austria, League, 1956

Hans Krankel (Rapid Vienna) v GAK, Austria, League, 1976

Hugh Maxwell (Falkirk) v. Clyde, League, 1962

Billy Minter (St Albans City) v. Dulwich Hamlet, FA Cup, 1922*

Sven Nielsen (Denmark) v. France 'A', Olympic Games, London, 1908

Refik Resmja (Partizani) v. Tomori, Albanian League, 1951

Jimmy Ross (Preston North End) v. Hyde, FA Cup, 1887

Bob Thomson (Chelsea) v. Luton Town, London Combination, 1916

Albert Whitehurst (Bradford City) v. Tranmere Rovers, League, 1930

Vivian Woodward (England) v. France, amateur international, 1906

Harold Bache (England) v. France, Amateur International, 1910

+ Dyet was making his debut in first-class football.

* Minter was on the losing side – 8-7.

Other Hot Shots

Lothar Emmerich scored six goals for Borussia Dortmund *v.* Floriana (Malta) in a European Cup-Winners' Cup game in 1965 – the most by one player in a competitive European game.

Frankie Bunn of Oldham Athletic netted a record six goals in a League Cup tie against Scarborough in October 1989.

Around the World

Alfredo Di Stefano scored 424 goals in his first 500 competitive games up to September 1962. Of these, 23 were penalties, 22 came from direct free-kicks, 75 were headers and 304 were shots or tap-ins.

Artur Friedenreich (a Brazilian) holds the record for scoring most senior goals in a career. He netted 1,329 over a period of twenty years between 1910 and 1930.

Pelé (also a Brazilian) netted 1,283 goals in twenty-two years between 1956 and 1978.

Franz 'Bimbo' Binder (who played in Austria and Germany) claimed 1,006 goals in his twenty-year career (1930-1950).

Individual Records
& Personal Achievements

Jimmy McGrory retired in 1938 with a total of 550 competitive goals to his name, of which 468 were scored in 445 League and cup games for Celtic, whom he served from 1921. McGrory netted 410 goals in 408 League games, with 397 coming in 378 games in two spells for the Bhoys.

Arthur Rowley scored a career total of 434 League goals while serving with four clubs. The first four were scored in the Second Division for West Bromwich Albion in 1948. His last came as a Shrewsbury Town player in 1965. He scored in each of Fulham's last seven Second Division matches in season 1948/49 and was Leicester City's leading marksman eight seasons running from 1950/51 to 1957/58. His overall tally of 265 goals in 321 senior games for the Foxes remains a club record.

Following Rowley and McGrory in the career scoring stakes, we have Hughie Gallacher, who netted 387 goals in League football for seven different clubs between 1921 and 1939. Dixie Dean comes next with a total of 379 League goals, secured with Tranmere Rovers, Everton and Notts County. Hugh Ferguson hit 363 while playing for Motherwell, Cardiff City and Dundee (1916-1930). He claimed 362 in all games for the 'Well. Jimmy Greaves notched 357, all in the First Division with Chelsea, Spurs and West Ham (1957-1971). Cradley Heath-born striker Steve Bloomer scored 352 for Derby County and Middlesbrough (1892-1914). Centre forward George Camsell (Durham City and Middlesbrough) weighed in with 345 (1923-1939). David Halliday, who assisted St Mirren, Dundee, Sunderland, Arsenal, Manchester City and Clapton Orient, amassed 336 in fourteen years from 1921 to 1935. Vic Watson of West Ham United and Southampton fame struck 317 between 1920 and 1936 and John Atyeo fired home 315, all for Bristol City, between 1951 and 1966.

Alan Shearer netted the 350th goal of his club career for Newcastle United against West Bromwich Albion in the Premiership in September 2004. Alan also scored 30 goals for England.

Fred Roberts, centre forward of Glentoran, scored 96 goals in 1930/31, including 55 in the Irish League and 28 in the Belfast City Cup. Joe Bambrick of Linfield had netted 94 the previous season, including 50 in the Irish League.

The top scorer in one season of Scottish football is Jock Smith of Ayr United who claimed 84 goals in 1927/28 (66 in the Second Division).

Dixie Dean scored 81 goals in season 1927/28. He hit 60 in the Football League and 3 in the FA Cup for Everton, 6 in inter-league games, 8 in international trial matches and 4 for the full England team. He scored 17 in the first 9 League games, netting in each one, and finished off with 17 in the last 8. He also found the net in 12 consecutive games between December and February when he scored in 15 out of 16 matches including FA Cup ties. He totalled 29 goals in the latter sequence.

Joe Payne was playing his first senior game at centre forward when he scored ten goals for Bristol Rovers in their 12-0 League win over Luton Town on 13 April 1936. In fact, he was not even mentioned in the matchday programme line-up.

Derek Dooley scored 63 goals in only 63 first-class games for Sheffield Wednesday before a broken leg (which led to an amputation) ended his career in 1953.

Jock Dodds netted 65 goals in only 32 games for Blackpool in wartime regional league and cup competitions in 1941/42.

Stan Lynn scored 70 goals in senior football during his playing career with Accrington Stanley, Aston Villa and Birmingham City. His tally of 64 in League football is a record for a full-back.

Steve Bloomer was leading scorer for Derby County on fourteen occasions, for seasons 1892/93 to 1905/06 – a Football League record.

George Camsell topped Middlesbrough's scoring charts in ten successive seasons, 1926-1936. He scored in 12 consecutive League games, a run that comprised 29 goals, in 1926/27.

Jack Milsom was Bolton Wanderers' leading scorer six seasons running from 1931/32 to 1936/37.

During the late 1960s and early 1970s, Jim Fryatt scored League goals for Oldham Athletic against four of his previous clubs: Southend United, Southport, Stockport County and Torquay United.

Chester scored 154 goals in the 1964/65 season – 119 in the Fourth Division and 35 in 6 cup games.

Denis Law scored four goals at Wembley for three different teams against the same goalkeeper, Gordon Banks. He was on target for Manchester United v. Leicester City in the 1963 FA Cup final, for the Rest of the World against England that same year and for Scotland v. England in the Home International matches in 1965 and 1967.

Centre forward Terry Bly scored 55 goals for Peterborough United in their first season of League football, 1960/61.

In 2002/03 Alan Shearer became the first player to score a century of Premiership goals for two different clubs (Blackburn Rovers and Newcastle United). He also equalled the fastest-ever Premiership goal and claimed his first European hat-trick for the St James' Park side. Earlier, in April 2002, playing for Newcastle against Charlton, he became the first player to score 200 Premiership goals. Alan retired with 260 goals to his credit.

Gilbert Alsop, Walsall's centre forward, was the only player to score 40 goals in season in both the Third Division (South) and Third Division (North), a feat he achieved in 1933/34 and 1934/35.

Les Ferdinand had the pleasure of scoring the 10,000th Premiership goal, for Tottenham Hotspur against Fulham on 15 December 2001. Brian Deane scored the first in August 1992 for Sheffield United against Manchester United.

Middlesbrough's George Camsell netted 29 goals in 12 Second Division games between October 1926 and New Year's Day 1927. His tally included a five-goal haul, three fours and one hat-trick. He ended that season with 59 goals in 37 games.

Liverpool's Phil Boersma scored in four different competitions in the space of thirty-seven days in August and September 1974: the FA Charity Shield, First Division, League Cup and European Cup-Winners' Cup.

Left-winger Roly Bartholomew scored only one League goal for Bradford City in 1937/38, but in 5 FA Cup games he netted 7 times.

Bobby Smith scored six goals at Wembley in 1960/61 – five for England and one for Spurs. All six were netted at the same end of the ground, to the right of the Royal Box.

When Oldham Athletic beat Newton-le-Willows 11-0 in a Lancashire Combination 'B' Division game in January 1905, Jack Plumpton scored the first five goals and Jim Sheridan the last six.

Ian Rush's first League goal for Liverpool was scored past Arsenal's John Lukic in 1981. His 200th, in 1993, was against the same 'keeper, then of Leeds United.

Queen's Park (Glasgow) did not concede a goal between 1867 and 1874.

Jim Glazzard scored four headed goals, all from left-wing crosses by Vic Metcalfe, when Huddersfield Town beat Everton 8-2 in a Second Division game at Leeds Road in April 1953. Glazzard later moved to Goodison Park.

Colin Garwood ended the 1979/80 season as leading scorer for both Aldershot and Portsmouth.

Tommy Spratt, aged sixteen, scored 14 goals in a 25-0 win when making his debut for Manchester United's fifth team in 1957/58.

Yeovil Town scored an incredible 225 goals (81 away) in all competitions during season 1931/32.

In January 2003, both Dennis Bergkamp and Thierry Henry scored their 100th goals for Arsenal.

Aston Villa's Dion Dublin scored his 100th Premiership goal in November 2002 and the following month netted his 200th overall (in all competitions).

Future PFA chairman Gordon Taylor scored 97 goals in one season of schoolboy football before joining Bolton Wanderers as a sixteen-year-old in 1960.

During October and November 1898, Birmingham scored 35 goals without reply in 4 competitive games. They beat Chirk 8-0 and Druids 10-0 in the FA Cup and crushed Luton Town 9-0 and Darwen 8-0 in League encounters.

One of the fastest goals ever scored at Wembley came in a schoolboy international between England and Wales in 1957, struck home by Derek Woodley of Southend United after just thirteen seconds in England's 2-0 win. Another fast Wembley goal, netted after only twenty seconds, was recorded in the annual Varsity match of 1979 and was scored by Maurice Cox for Cambridge against Oxford.

Two Aston Villa defenders, centre half Frank Barson (against Sheffield United in 1921) and full-back Peter Aldis (against Sunderland in 1952), headed League goals from distances of over thirty yards. Ian Edwards headed a thirty-five-yard goal in a Central League game for West Bromwich Albion reserves v. Liverpool reserves in March 1974.

Centre forward Freddie Roberts scored 96 goals for Glentoran in the 1930/31 season.

Ronnie Allen (Port Vale, West Bromwich Albion and Crystal Palace) is the only player to have scored in the League and/or FA Cup in twenty successive post-Second World War seasons: 1945/46 to 1964/65 inclusive. He also netted for Vale in 1944/45.

Stanley Matthews scored his first League goal for Stoke City in March 1933 and his last for the same club thirty years later in May 1963. Matthews' first goal for England was scored in 1937, his last nineteen years later in 1956.

Other players with long spans between their first and last League goals include Jackie Carr (1910-1932, his first for Middlesbrough, his last for Hartlepool United); Billy Gillespie (1910-1930, for Leeds City and Sheffield United); Alec Herd (1929-1950, for Hamilton Academical and Stockport County); Bob Kelly (1913-1934, for Burnley and Carlisle United); Syd Puddefoot (1913-1933, for West Ham United) and Billy Smith (1913-1934, for Huddersfield Town).

Eight different players figured on the scoresheet when Crewe Alexandra beat Hartlepool United 8-0 in an Auto Windscreens Shield game in October 1995.

Aston Villa scored thirteen goals against rivals Birmingham City in the space of six weeks between September to November 1988. They won 2-0 and 5-0 in home and away League Cup games and 6-0 in a Simod Cup tie.

Spurs striker Les Ferdinand (v. Fulham in 2001) scored the 10,000th goal in Premiership football while Moritz Volz of Fulham netted the 15,000th goal v. Chelsea in 2006.

Fast Scoring

George James for West Bromwich Albion against Nottingham Forest in 1925, Albert Mundy for Aldershot at Hartlepool United in 1958, Barrie Jones on his debut for Notts County against Torquay United in 1962, Keith Smith for Crystal Palace *v.* Derby County in 1964 and Jim Fryatt for Bradford Park Avenue against Tranmere Rovers in 1964 are all credited with having scored a goal between the fourth and sixth seconds of a League game, with Fryatt's the fastest on record at just over four seconds (confirmed by referee Mr R.J. Simon)

Willie Sharp scored in just under seven seconds for Partick Thistle against Queen of the South in a Scottish League 'A' game in 1947 – the fastest north of the border.

Two players have scored a goal after just seven seconds: winger Bobby Langton for Preston North End against Manchester City in August 1948 and Ray Drake for Stockport County against Accrington Stanley in December 1956.

Keith East of Bournemouth (against Shrewsbury Town in 1968) and George Hudson for Tranmere Rovers (against Bury in 1967) both scored League goals inside eight seconds.

In February 2004, Bournemouth substitute James Hayter came on in the eighty-fifth minute and scored a hat-trick in just 140 seconds against Wrexham to set a new Football League record.

Three players have scored four goals in five minutes in League football: John McIntyre for Blackburn Rovers at home to Everton in September 1922, W.G. Richardson for West Bromwich Albion at West Ham in November 1931 and Willie Best for Rangers against Arbroath in November 1968. Richardson's foursome came between the fourth and ninth minutes in a 5-1 win.

George Stobbart netted four times in eight minutes for Luton Town against Blackburn Rovers in November 1949.

Gary Shaw (Shrewsbury Town) scored three goals in 167 seconds in a 4-2 League win over Bradford City in December 1990.

Players who have scored three goals in three minutes in League games include Johnny Hartburn for Leyton Orient *v.* Shrewsbury Town, January 1955; Billy Lane for Watford against Clapton Orient, December 1933; winger Graham Leggatt for Fulham against Ipswich Town, Boxing Day, 1963 (the Cottagers won 10-1); John Lindsay for Southport *v.* Scunthorpe United, February 1952; Jimmy McGrory for Celtic *v.* Motherwell, March 1936 and Jack Scarth for Gillingham *v.* Leyton Orient, November 1952.

Ian St John scored a hat-trick in three minutes playing in a Scottish League Cup tie for Motherwell against Hibernian in August 1959. Jack Swindells of Altrincham scored three goals in three minutes during an FA Cup tie against Scarborough in November 1965, as did Gary Talbot for Chester against Crewe Alexandra in November 1964.

Nigel Clough scored three goals in four minutes (eighty-first to eighty-fifth) for Nottingham Forest against QPR in December 1987.

Brian Dear claimed five goals in twenty first-half minutes for West Ham United against West Bromwich Albion in April 1965.

Frank Keetley scored six goals in twenty-one minutes for Lincoln City against Halifax Town in a League game in January 1932.

Tottenham Hotspur players scored three goals in 154 seconds (between the fifth and eighth minutes) against Oldham Athletic in September 1993. Spurs won 5-0.

Preston players scored six goals in seven minutes when they defeated Hyde 26-0 in an FA Cup tie in 1887. Every player except the goalkeeper scored in this game.

Grounds

A soccer mystery that has never been cleared up occurred on 30 April 1921 when there was an epidemic of fire outbreaks during Football League matches at many different grounds including Burnley, Bradford Park Avenue, Nottingham Forest and Preston North End.

Queens Park Rangers have played competitive home matches on twelve different grounds.

The Maracana Stadium in Rio de Janiero, Brazil, had a capacity of 200,000 in 1950.

The Hawthorns, home of West Bromwich Albion, is the highest Football League ground above sea level in Britain at 551 feet. Union Minas of Peru play at the world's highest senior ground – 15,200 feet above sea level – while non-League Tow Law's ground is effectively the highest above sea level in the United Kingdom at 560 feet.

Of all the current League clubs, Preston North End have been at their Deepdale ground the longest – since 1881. Deepdale has in fact been a sporting venue since 1875.

Eighty-nine normal strides separate the boundary wall of Dundee's Dens Park ground from that of Tannadice Park, home of their near neighbours Dundee United – the closest pair of grounds in senior football in Great Britain.

The Vetch Field, former home of Swansea City, was formerly a disused gasworks dump that the Welsh club rented from the local gas company.

half-time scores

Preston North End led Hyde 10-0 at half-time before going on to win 26-0 in an FA Cup tie in October 1887.

Norwich City were also 10-0 up at the interval in their home Wartime Regional League South game with Brighton & Hove Albion on Christmas Day 1940. The Canaries won 18-0.

Arsenal, 8-0 up on Darwen in a home third round FA Cup tie in January 1932, went on to win 11-1.

On 4 March 1933, Coventry City went in at half-time of their Third Division (South) game against QPR leading by 7-0. That was the final score.

The half-time scoreline of the 1927 Boxing Day League game between Luton Town and Northampton Town was 5-0 in favour of the Hatters. The final result was Luton 5 Northampton 6 – the most amazing transformation in Football League history.

Southport trailed Everton 7-0 at half-time in their sixth round FA Cup tie in 1931. The Toffees ran out 9-1 winners.

The record away win in the old Second Division was 10-0, achieved by Sheffield United on a snowbound pitch in front of 500 hardy fans at Burslem Port Vale in December 1892. At half-time United led 5-0, having scored four times in a six-minute spell at the start of the contest.

Sheffield United led Birmingham 6-0 at the interval of their First Division game in February 1923. The final score was 7-1.

Eight goals, 6-2 in favour of the home side Middlesbrough, were scored in the first half of their game with Sheffield United in November 1933. Boro won 10-3.

When Newcastle United beat Newport County 13-0 in a home Second Division match in October 1946, they led 7-0 at the interval.

The scoresheet was blank as the players left the field at half-time in the League game between Exeter City and Aldershot at St James' Park in 1934/35. The final score was Exeter 8 Aldershot 1.

Sheffield Wednesday (7-0 up at half-time) defeated the ten men of Sunderland 8-0 in a home League game on Boxing Day 1911.

Hat-tricks

League/Premiership

The first Premiership hat-trick was scored by Mick Quinn for Coventry City v. Arsenal on 14 August 1993.

Fred Howard scored a hat-trick in the first thirteen minutes of his League debut for Manchester City v. Liverpool in January 1913. He later added a fourth goal as City won 4-1.

Aston Villa's Harry Nash also scored a hat-trick on his League debut against Liverpool in April 1915. Villa won 6-2.

5ft 5in Craig Midgley scored a hat-trick of headed goals for Hartlepool United against Barnet in December 2000.

Fred Whitlow of Exeter City scored nine League hat-tricks in two seasons: 1931/32 and 1932/33.

Charlie Wilson scored a hat-trick for Huddersfield in both League games against Arsenal in 1923/24 – a 3-1 win at Highbury and a 6-1 victory at Leeds Road.

David Mercer scored a double hat-trick for Hull City against Sheffield United in January 1919. In December 1920 he was transferred from the Tigers to Bramall Lane for £4,500.

Johnny Goodall of Preston North End was the first player to score hat-tricks in consecutive League games – against Wolves (won 5-2) and Notts County (won 7-0) in October/November 1888.

Frank Osborne scored hat-tricks for Spurs in three consecutive First Division matches in October and November 1925.

Tom Jennings of Leeds United scored hat-tricks in three successive matches in September/October 1926, against Arsenal (three goals), Liverpool (four goals) and Blackburn Rovers (four goals).

Barney Battles of Hearts also claimed three trebles in succession in November 1930, against Motherwell, Dundee and St Mirren.

In November 1946, Liverpool's Jack Balmer also netted a hat-trick of hat-tricks in games against Portsmouth (three goals), Derby County (four goals) and Arsenal (three goals) in successive First Division matches.

Robert Taylor netted five goals for Gillingham at Burnley in February 1999, including a hat-trick in just seven minutes.

Fred Smith scored four goals in seven minutes (between the fourteenth and twenty-first) for Grimsby Town against Hartlepool United in the Third Division (North) in November 1952.

On 4 November 1911, Billy Halligan scored a hat-trick for Wolves in an 8-0 home League win over Hull City. Two years later he scored four goals for Hull in a 7-1 win over Wolves.

Robbie Fowler scored a Premiership hat-trick in four minutes thirty-three seconds for Liverpool against Arsenal in August 1994.

Jock Dodds for Lincoln City against West Ham United, in 1948, David Herd for Manchester United v. Sunderland in 1966, Brian Clark for Bournemouth v. Rotherham United in 1974, Alvin Martin for West Ham United against Newcastle

United in 1986 and Chris Pike for Hereford United against Colchester United (who had two 'keepers sent off) all scored hat-tricks against three different goalkeepers.

Brian Clough scored eight goals for Middlesbrough against Brighton & Hove Albion in 1958/59 – five in a 9-0 home win and a hat-trick in a 6-4 away victory. Clough also netted trebles in both League games against Scunthorpe United that same season.

The first out-and-out winger to score a hat-trick on his League debut was Jimmy Randall for Ashington against Nelson in a Third Division (North) game in August 1925.

Colin Viljoen scored a hat-trick on his League debut for Ipswich Town against Portsmouth in March 1967.

Tom Peacock scored four goals in a game on three occasions in the space of seven weeks for Nottingham Forest during November and December 1935.

Ron Saunders scored a hat-trick for Portsmouth in the two League games against Leyton Orient in 1963/64. Pompey won 6-3 at home and 4-3 away.

Hugh McIlmoyle scored two headed hat-tricks for Carlisle United in October and December 1963 against Hartlepool United and Tranmere Rovers.

Two seasons later, in 1965/66, Huddersfield Town's Les Massie did likewise against Middlesbrough, the Terriers winning 6-0 at home and 3-1 away.

Jim Hall with four goals and Peter Price with three were hat-trick heroes for Peterborough United in an 8-1 win over Oldham Athletic in November 1969. Two years later, in October 1971, they again both netted hat-tricks when Posh beat Barrow 7-0.

In September 1969, Fulham's Steve Earle scored five goals in his side's 8-0 away win at Halifax Town and followed up with a hat-trick in a 4-2 defeat of Stockport County at Edgeley Park.

Wyn Davies, Ron Barnes and Roy Ambler all netted hat-tricks for Wrexham in a 10-1 Fourth Division victory over Hartlepool United in March 1962.

When Manchester City beat Huddersfield Town 10-1 in a Second Division game at Maine Road in November 1987, there were also three hat-trick heroes: David White, Paul Stewart and Tony Adcock.

In November 1947, Sunderland's Ronnie Turnbull celebrated his Football League First Division debut with a four-goal haul against Portsmouth.

Terry Allcock is one of the few players to score a hat-trick against Liverpool at Anfield, doing so for Norwich City in a Second Division game in January 1962. The Merseysiders still won 5-4.

Geoff Vowden was the first substitute to score a League hat-trick, doing so for Birmingham City against Huddersfield Town in the Second Division) in September 1968.

Full-back Stan Lynn of Aston Villa was the first full-back to score a hat-trick in a First Division game, against Sunderland in January 1958. Bobby Cram (West Bromwich Albion) repeated the feat against Stoke City in September 1964. Some years earlier, Jack Brownsword of Scunthorpe United was the first full-back to record a hat-trick in a League game.

Tom Nicol scored a hat-trick (some reports say four goals) on his debut for Burnley against Preston North End at Turf Moor in March 1891. Burnley won 6-2.

In 1926/27 Middlesbrough centre forward George Camsell registered eighteen hat-tricks – a record for a single season in the Football League.

Cliff Holton scored hat-tricks on consecutive days for Watford in 1960.

John O'Rourke was the first player to score hat-tricks in all four divisions of the Football League, doing so for Luton Town (Fourth Division) in 1965/66, for

Middlesbrough (Third Division) in 1966/67 and 1967/68 (Second Division) and for Coventry City (First Division) in 1969/70.

Arthur Rowley scored a hat-trick for Leicester City in both League games against his former club Fulham in season 1952/53.

Cup Trebles

The fastest hat-trick in FA Cup history was scored in just four minutes fifty-four seconds by Barnet's Wayne Purser against Havant & Waterlooville in November 2001.

Burnley's Ian Lawson recorded a four-goal haul and a hat-trick in his first two FA Cup ties, against Chesterfield in round three and New Brighton in round four in January 1957.

Kevin Davies scored Chesterfield's first ever FA Cup hat-trick, against Bolton Wanderers, in February 1997, and the 3-2 victory took the Spireites into the fifth round of the competition for the first time. Davies joined Bolton in July 2003.

Three players, Les Allen (five goals), Bobby Smith (four) and Cliff Jones (three), scored hat-tricks for Spurs in their 13-2 home FA Cup win over Crewe Alexandra in January 1960.

Norwich City star Terry Allcock was the first player to net a hat-trick in League, FA Cup and League Cup competitions (1962 and 1963).

To celebrate his twenty-first birthday, David Gwyther headed four goals for Swansea in an FA Cup tie against Oxford City in 1969. He also scored hat-tricks in three other cup matches against non-League opponents when striking for Halifax Town against Telford United and Rhyl in 1970 and Frickley in 1973.

Ian St John scored a second-half hat-trick in 145 seconds for Motherwell against Hibernian in an away Scottish League Cup tie in August 1959. The 'Well won 3-1.

Three Walsall players, Tom Johnson (four goals), Alf Griffin (three) and George Johnson (three), scored hat-tricks in an 11-0 FA Cup qualifying round win over Dresden United in November 1896.

Ian Callaghan played in all of Liverpool's 61 competitive games in 1973/74 and scored 3 goals – a hat-trick against Hull City in a League Cup tie.

Joe Harper scored a hat-trick for Hibernian against Celtic in the 1974 Scottish Cup final yet still finished up on the losing side in a 6-3 defeat.

The last player to score a hat-trick in an FA Cup semi-final was Alex Dawson for Manchester United against Fulham in the Highbury replay of 1958.

European/Foreign Heroes

Kevin Hector (five goals), Leighton James (three) and Charlie George (three) were hat-trick heroes for Derby County in a 12-0 UEFA Cup win over Finn Harps in September 1976.

Ferenc Puskas is the only player so far to have scored hat-tricks in two European Cup finals.

Extrovert Paraguayan goalkeeper Jose Luis Chilavert scored a hat-trick in a League game for Velez Sarsfield against Ferro Carrilk Oeste in November 1999. He ended his career with over 50 senior goals to his credit – a record for a 'keeper anywhere in the world.

International Hat-tricks

Dennis Wilshaw (Wolves) was the first player to score four goals in a full international match at Wembley, doing so for England against Scotland in April 1955. The English won 7-2.

Malcolm Macdonald scored all of England's goals when they beat Cyprus 5-0 at Wembley in a European Championship qualifier in April 1975.

Treble Chance

Ted Hartson scored eleven hat-tricks for Mansfield Town over two seasons: 1935/36 and 1936/37. His tally included a seven-goal haul in an 8-2 home win over Hartlepool United in January 1937. He also scored three goals in the first seven minutes of a League game against Southport in October 1935.

Joe Bradford scored three hat-tricks in eight days during September 1929 – two for his club Birmingham, against Newcastle United and Blackburn Rovers, and one for the Football League against the Irish League.

By scoring a hat-trick against Bolton Wanderers on 13 September 1997, Ian Wright took his total of League and Cup goals for Arsenal to 179 – a current club record.

John Jepson scored three hat-tricks for Accrington Stanley against Wrexham in 1925/26 – two in Third Division (North) games and one in the FA Cup. Stanley won all three games, 6-5 at home, 4-2 away and 4-0 at home respectively.

Fred Pickering scored hat-tricks for four different Everton teams in 1963/64, also netting three times on his England debut at the end of that season in a 10-0 win over the USA.

On the morning of 20 February 1922, Billy Pontz got married. In the afternoon he went out and scored a hat-trick for Leeds United against Leicester at Elland Road.

During the 1960s and 1970s, England international Tony Brown scored hat-tricks for West Bromwich Albion in the First Division, Second Division, FA Cup, League Cup, Fairs Cup and Central League, as well as in friendlies.

In his career (for Portsmouth and Ipswich Town) Ray Crawford netted hat-tricks in First, Second and Fourth Division matches, in the FA Cup and League Cup and also in the European Cup.

Birmingham City's Scottish-born outside left Alex Govan scored four hat-tricks during the 1956/57 season.

Jack Shepherd scored four goals on his debut for Millwall v. Leyton Orient in October 1952. He then followed up with hat-tricks against Shrewsbury Town (League) and Aldershot and Barrow in the FA Cup during the next 10 matches.

Dixie Dean scored thirty-seven hat-tricks for Everton – thirty-four in the League – and two for England.

Injuries

Much-travelled centre forward Frank Lord, whose clubs included Rochdale, Crewe Alexandra, Plymouth Argyle, Stockport County, Blackburn Rovers and Chesterfield, sustained more injuries than most players during his career. He was treated for three fractured legs, four broken fingers, a broken arm, cracked ribs, a fractured jaw, a dislocated elbow, a chipped anklebone, numerous facial cuts that required stitches and concussion. A hard man!

Full-back Albert Evans broke his leg five times during his footballing career: in 1901 when playing for Aston Villa against Stoke; in 1903 when attempting to jump

over a culvert when out for a walk; in 1906 playing for Villa's reserve side; in 1908 when defending for West Bromwich Albion against Gainsborough Trinity and lastly in 1912 when playing in a local charity match!

Bryan Robson broke his leg three times in the same season, 1976/77, when registered with West Bromwich Albion.

In August 1966, Bobby Blackwood fractured his jaw in two places playing for Colchester United against QPR. The player he collided with was Les Allen. Four months later, in the return fixture, Blackwood broke his jaw again after another clash with Allen!

During a League game between Chester and Aldershot in January 1966 the two Chester full-backs, both named Jones, broke legs.

International Football

England

Aston Villa's Howard Vaughton scored five goals on his international debut for England against Ireland in 1882.

Apart from Vaughton only three other players have scored five goals in a full international for England: Steve Bloomer (Derby County) v. Wales in 1896, Willie Hall (Tottenham Hotspur) v. Ireland in 1938 and Malcolm Macdonald (Newcastle United) v. Cyprus in 1975.

Arthur Brown (Aston Villa) v. Ireland in 1882 and Stan Mortensen (Blackpool) v. Portugal in 1947, both claimed four goals when making their England debuts.

The England team v. Wales at Wrexham in March 1894 and at the Queen's Club, London in March 1895, comprised eleven players who had all previously appeared or were with the famous amateur side Corinthians.

Wolves provided the England half-back line in four consecutive internationals in May and June 1958: Eddie Clamp, Billy Wright and Bill Slater v. USSR (twice), Brazil and Austria.

Tommy Lawton was the only player to appear for England in their last international match before the Second World War and their first after it. In fact, Lawton, Stanley Matthews and Raich Carter were the only players to represent England before and after the war.

Middlesbrough centre forward George Camsell scored in each of his nine full international games for England between May 1929 and April 1936. He netted 18 goals in all.

England beat West Germany 2-0 in the 100th international staged at Wembley, in 1975.

Viv Anderson was the first black player to win a full cap for England, against Czechoslovakia in 1978, Luther Blissett was the first black player to score for

England, against Luxembourg in October 1982. West Bromwich Albion winger Laurie Cunningham was the first black player to represent England in an Under-21 international, v. Scotland at Bramall Lane, Sheffield, in 1977. Paul Ince was England's first black captain, against Brazil in 1993.

Bobby Charlton, with a total of 49, has scored the most senior goals for England.

A crowd of 80,529 at Hampden Park attended the 100th international between Scotland and England in 1982. Receipts amounted to over £500,000, compared with £103 for the first game between the two countries, which was staged at the West of Scotland cricket ground, Partick, on 30 November 1872.

Septimus Smith of Leicester City was the first player to appear as a substitute for England, replacing Manchester City's Jackie Bray in the second half of the Jubilee Fund game versus Scotland on 21 August 1935 at Hampden Park. The Scots won 4-2.

Norman Hunter of Leeds United became the first England player to win a cap as a substitute when he came on against Spain in 1965.

Jimmy Greaves scored four goals in an England international match on six occasions: against Norway in 1960, Luxembourg in 1960, Scotland in 1961, Peru in 1962 and Northern Ireland in 1963 and 1964.

When England beat Malta 5-0 at Wembley in 1971 there were no England goal kicks, no Maltese corner kicks and England goalkeeper Gordon Banks touched the ball just four times, all from back passes.

England remained unchanged for six consecutive internationals in 1966.

There were seven different goalscorers – an England record – when Luxembourg crashed 9-0 at Wembley in December 1982: Blissett (3), Woodcock, Coppell, Hoddle, Chamberlain, Neal and Bossi (own goal).

Everton had a complete team of England Under-23 internationals at the club in 1970/71: Gordon West, Tommy Wright, Keith Newton, Howard Kendall, Brian Labone, Henry Newton, Alan Ball, Joe Royle, John Hurst, Colin Harvey and Jimmy Husband.

Grimsby Town inside forward Jackie Bestall played for England only once but when he did – against Ireland in 1935 – he set three new records. Besides being the oldest player to gain his first cap (aged thirty-three), he was also the smallest at 5ft 2in and the lightest at 9st 2lbs.

Centre half Leslie Compton of Arsenal won his first England cap at the age of thirty-eight years sixty-four days, against Wales in November 1950.

Terry Venables was the first player to win international honours for England at five different levels: schoolboy, youth, amateur, Under-23 and full.

Hungary scored 13 goals in 2 internationals against England. They won 6-3 at Wembley in November 1953 and 7-1 in Budapest in May 1954. Birmingham City's Gil Merrick was the unlucky England goalkeeper in both matches.

There were seven Arsenal players in the England team that took on Italy in November 1934.

West Ham forward Jim Barrett's international career lasted for just five minutes. He was carried off injured when making his England debut against Ireland in 1929.

Aston Villa's Brian Little also had a short international career, coming on as a late substitute for his only cap against Wales in May 1975.

Wolves centre half Billy Wright made more Home International appearances than any other player – a total of 37. He also played in a then-record 13 consecutive internationals against Scotland (1947-1959), participated in 70 consecutive internationals, also a record (1951-1959) and captained his country 80 times in a total of 105 appearances.

Bobby Moore also acted as England's skipper in 80 games. He was just twenty-two when he tossed up for the first time in 1963.

Vivian Woodward won 23 amateur and 41 full caps for England (1908-1912) and also represented Great Britain in the 1908 Olympics. He netted seven against France in Paris in 1906 and six against Holland at Stamford Bridge, Chelsea, in 1909.

In May 1926, Willis Edwards of Leeds United became England's 500th capped player when he made his international debut at right half against Wales. Neil Webb of Nottingham Forest became the 1,000th player to win a full England cap when he starred against West Germany in September 1987.

Max Woosnam was capped by England at football, won the men's doubles tennis title at the 1920 Olympics and gained similar success at Wimbledon.

Chelsea and England goalkeeper Howard Baker also played cricket, was an accomplished swimmer, an Olympic-standard high jumper, pentathlete, Wimbledon tennis player and polo international.

George Eastham senior (1935) and George Eastham junior (1963-1966) both won full caps for England, as did Brian Clough (1959) and his son Nigel (1989-1993) and Frank Lampard (1972 and 1980) and son Frank junior (2000-present).

Edgar Kail of Dulwich Hamlet was the last non-League amateur to win a full cap for England, scoring twice on his debut at inside right v. France in Paris in 1929.

When England beat Wales 4-1 in 1953, all five goals came from headers.

Spurs' Willie Hall scored a hat-trick for England against Northern Ireland in 1938 in 210 seconds, between the thirty-fourth and thirty-eighth minutes.

Andy Cole and Nick Barmby were the first two graduates from the FA National School to win full caps for England, both as substitutes against Uruguay in 1993.

The first full international match played on an artificial pitch was between the USA and England in Detroit in 1993.

England have played two full internationals on the same day on three occasions: on 15 March 1880 v. Wales and Ireland; on 7 March 1891 v. Wales and Ireland and on 5 March 1892, also v. Wales and Ireland. They won all six matches.

England went a record twenty games unbeaten between 1889 and 1896.

In 1895, Rabbi Powell became the only full-blooded Romany gypsy to play for England, scoring on his debut in a 9-0 win over Ireland at Derby.

Cradley Heath-born Steve Bloomer scored in ten successive internationals for England between 1895 and 1899. He netted 19 goals in total.

William Kenyon-Slaney was the first overseas player to win a full cap for England. He was born in India and played against Scotland in 1873.

England scored in fifty-two consecutive internationals between 1884 and 1901. Sheffield United's Ernest Needham missed a penalty in a 0-0 draw with Wales in 1902 to end the run.

Blackburn Rovers' James Forrest was the first professional to win a full cap for England, doing so against Scotland in 1885. He had turned 'pro' the year before.

Hungary, when winning 6-3 in November 1953, became the first continental team to beat England at Wembley, and indeed on home soil.

Four years earlier, the Republic of Ireland won 2-0 at Goodison Park to become the first foreign team to defeat England on home soil.

England's first defeat on foreign soil came in 1929 when they lost 4-3 to Spain.

The first time England played a Home International entirely under floodlights was against Northern Ireland (won 8-3) at Wembley on 20 November 1963.

Scotland

Scotland's first international was against England in 1872.

Scotland first suffered defeat at the hands of a continental team in 1950 when they lost 1-0 to Austria at Hampden Park.

Scotland players wore primrose and pink jerseys against England in 1900. The match became known as the 'Rosebery international.'

Lieutenant (later Colonel) Henry Waugh Renney-Tailyour, who was born in Mussoorie, North West Province, India, played for Scotland at both rugby and association football in 1872 and 1873. Also a county cricketer for Kent (1873-1883) and a champion athlete, he was later managing director of the Guinness company from 1913 to 1919. He won the FA Cup with the Royal Engineers in 1875.

Denis Law and Kenny Dalglish, with thirty goals each, share the honour of having scored the most international goals for Scotland. Dalglish has also played in the most full internationals for his country (102).

Hugh Gallacher has the record for scoring the most goals in an international match for Scotland, netting five against Ireland in Belfast in September 1929. The Scots won 7-3.

Aberdeen and Scotland goalkeeper Fred Martin conceded seven goals against Uruguay in the 1954 World Cup finals and against England at Wembley a year later.

Manchester United's Denis Law scored four goals for Scotland at Hampden Park in successive years, against Northern Ireland in November 1962 and Norway in November 1963.

Andy Watson was the first black player to win a cap for Scotland, against England in 1881.

Ireland and Northern Ireland

Ireland's first full international was against England at Bloomfield, Belfast on 16 February 1882. The score was a resounding 13-0 win for England, two Aston Villa players, Brown and Vaughton, sharing nine goals.

Linfield's Joe Bambrick holds the Northern Ireland record for scoring most goals in an international match, netting six against Wales in Belfast in 1930.

Northern Ireland played 1,298 minutes of international football without scoring, their goal drought ending in 2003/04.

Goalkeeper Pat Jennings, with a total of 119, has gained the most caps at senior level for Northern Ireland.

With 36 to his name, David Healy (Sunderland) and has netted the most international goals for Northern Ireland.

Norman Whiteside was only seventeen years forty-two days old when he made his international debut for Northern Ireland v. Yugoslavia in June 1982.

Republic of Ireland

In the space of three days, 28-30 September 1946, Manchester United defender Johnny Carey played against England twice for different countries – for Northern Ireland and the Republic of Ireland respectively.

When Everton's Peter Farrell scored for the Republic of Ireland in an historic 2-0 win over England at Goodison Park in September 1949, he became the first international to score an away goal on his home ground. This international saw England suffer their first home defeat by an overseas country.

The Republic of Ireland's champion marksman at the time of writing (2005) is Robbie Keane, who passed Niall Quinn's tally of 21 goals (in 91 games) in October 2004 when he scored twice in a World Cup qualifier against the Faroe Islands.

Two players – Don Givens (v. Turkey in 1975) and Paddy Moore (v. Belgium in 1934) – have scored four goals in an international match for Eire.

Steve Staunton, with 102, has won the most international caps for the Republic of Ireland.

Jimmy Holmes was seventeen years 200 days old when he made his full international debut for the Republic against Austria in 1971 – his country's youngest player.

Wales

Wales played their first international match against Scotland in Glasgow in 1876. The Scots won 4-0.

Ian Rush holds the record for scoring the most goals for Wales, 28 in 73 full internationals between 1980 and 1996.

The first substitute used in a Home International by Wales was Allen Pugh of Rostyllen who took over from injured goalkeeper Samuel Gladstone Gillam against Scotland at Wrexham in 1889.

The first Fourth Division player to win a full cap for Wales was Vic Rouse of Crystal Palace, against Northern Ireland in 1959.

All five forwards in the Welsh team against Ireland in 1953 – Terry Medwin, John Charles, Trevor Ford, Ivor Allchurch and Harry Griffiths – were born in Swansea and had played for Swansea Town.

In season 1981/82 nine Swansea City players won full caps for Wales.

Stan Davies, who played for Everton, West Bromwich Albion and Birmingham among other clubs, was capped by Wales in six different positions, even going in goal during one game.

Three players have scored four goals in an international match for Wales: John Price of Wrexham against Ireland in 1882; Mel Charles of Cardiff City against Northern Ireland in 1962 and Ian Edwards of Chester against Malta in 1978.

On Wednesday 28 September 1934, Ron Williams appeared in Newcastle United's third team in a Tyneside League game in front of barely a hundred spectators. Three days later he was centre forward for Wales in the Home International Championship match against England at Ninian Park, Cardiff, where the crowd was 51,000.

The Welsh team that took on Northern Ireland in Belfast in April 1959 contained players from all four divisions of the Football League. Besides seven from First Division clubs, there were Derek Sullivan and Derek Tapscott (Cardiff City) from the Second Division, Tony Rowley (Tranmere Rovers) from the Third Division and Vic Rouse (Crystal Palace) from the Fourth Division.

The first black player to appear in a Home International match was Eddie Parris of Bradford, who represented Wales against Ireland in 1931. He was the son of a West Indian father and a Welsh mother.

Goalkeeper Neville Southall has been capped the most times by Wales, appearing on 92 occasions between 1983 and 1997.

Ryan Giggs was only seventeen years 332 days old when he made his debut for Wales, against Germany in 1991. In contrast, fellow winger Billy Meredith was forty-five years 229 days when he played in his last international for Wales, v. England in 1920.

Overseas

The Australian Archie Thompson of Marconi Stallions holds the individual scoring record for the most goals in an international match – thirteen in his country's amazing 31-0 win over American Samoa (effectively a youth team) in New South Wales on 11 April 2001.

The 1967/68 European Nations Cup semi-final between Italy and USSR was decided by the toss of a coin. The Italians won in their own country.

One famous 'Magical Magyar', inside right Sandor Kocsis, scored 75 goals in 68 full internationals for Hungary between 1948 and 1956.

While attaining European Footballer of the Year status in 1957 and 1959, Alfredo Di Stefano played international football for Argentina, Spain and Colombia. Ladislav Kubala played for Hungary, Czechoslovakia and Spain.

Goalkeeper Joe Kennaway was also capped by three different countries: Canada, USA and Scotland, the latter after joining Celtic in 1931.

Players who have gained full international honours with different countries (some of whom are mentioned elsewhere in this book) include Ferenc Puskas (Hungary and Spain), Jose Altafina (Brazil and Italy), Luis Monti (Argentina and Italy), Omar Sivori (Argentina and Italy), Jose Emilio Santamaria (Uruguay and Spain), Juan Alberto Schiaffino (Uruguay and Italy), Jack 'Baldy' Reynolds (England and Ireland) and Robert Evans (England and Wales).

Reynolds, who played for Aston Villa, Celtic, West Bromwich Albion and Southampton, won 5 caps for Ireland and later collected 8 more with England. Evans was capped 10 times by Wales (1906-1910) and represented England 4 times before the First World War.

Spain beat Malta 12-1 in a European Championship game in 1983, the biggest international score featuring two European countries.

Denmark beat France 17-1 in an Olympic Games encounter in 1908 and four years later, also in the Olympics, Germany defeated the USSR 16-0.

In another minor international, played in 1966, Libya beat Oman 21-0.

Internationally Speaking

In the 1998 World Cup finals, Chelsea had ten players appearing for various countries; four years later they had five.

Fulham's French manager Jean Tigana created history by fielding eleven internationals from eleven different countries against Bury in a home League Cup tie in November 2002.

In 1962/63 Spurs had eleven full internationals registered as professionals but they never played together as a team. They were Bill Brown (Scotland); Mel Hopkins (Wales), Ron Henry (England), Danny Blanchflower (Northern Ireland), Maurice Norman (England), Dave Mackay (Scotland), Terry Medwin (Wales), John White (Scotland), Bobby Smith (England), Jimmy Greaves (England) and Cliff Jones (Wales).

Three players who have scored with their first kick in full international football are Spurs' wing half Bill Nicholson for England against Portugal in 1951; Newcastle United winger Billy Foulkes for Wales against England, also in 1951, and Aston Villa outside left Peter McParland for Northern Ireland against Wales in 1954.

George Latham was the official trainer of Cardiff City and also the Welsh national team in 1913 but just prior to the start of a game against Ireland one of the chosen players was taken ill and Latham stepped up to win his tenth cap.

In February 1999, seven Arsenal players appeared in the international match between England and France (four English, three French).

In season 1925/26, Cardiff City had seventeen full internationals on their books – a record at that time.

Centre half Mike England won 44 caps for Wales between 1962 and 1975. In 1976 he played for Team America against England.

Brazil went 30 international matches without defeat before losing to France in April 1978.

Stuart McCall was selected for both the England and Scotland Under-21 sides in 1984.

Brentford's forward line in 1937/38 comprised five full internationals: Idris Hopkins (Wales), Bill Scott (England), Dave McCulloch (Scotland), George Eastham (England) and Bobby Reid (Scotland).

In 1968 a youth international in Rome between Italy and Malta attracted a crowd of 255 – 230 of whom were officials and newsmen. The gate receipts amounted to £20.

The first international match in Europe played without any British countries being involved was in October 1902 when Austria met Hungary.

Most Capped Players

Home Countries

125	Peter Shilton (England)
119	Pat Jennings (Northern Ireland)
108	Bobby Moore (England)
106	Bobby Charlton (England)
105	Billy Wright (England)
102	Kenny Dalglish (Scotland)
102	Steve Staunton (Republic of Ireland)
92	Neville Southall (Wales)

91	Jim Leighton (Scotland)
91	Niall Quinn (Republic of Ireland)
90	Bryan Robson (England)
88	Tony Cascarino (Republic of Ireland)
88	Sammy McIlroy (Northern Ireland)
88	Gary Speed (Wales)*
86	Kenny Sansom (England)
84	Ray Wilkins (England)
83	Paul McGrath (Republic of Ireland)
80	Gary Lineker (England)

* Still adding to total

Other players who have gained over 100 international caps include:

147	Hector Chumpitaz (Peru)
130	Majid Mohammed (Saudi Arabia)
129	Thomas Ravelli (Sweden)
128	Lothar Matthaus (Germany)
127	Andoni Zubizarreta (Spain)
120	Borislav Mikhailov (Bulgaria)
117	Heinz Hermann (Switzerland)
112	Dino Zoff (Italy)
106	Ladislav Bolini (Romania)
104	Franz Beckenbauer (Germany)
104	Grzegorz Lato (Poland)
104	Thorjan Svennsen (Norway)
104	Carlos Valderrama (Colombia)
102	Morten Olsen (Denmark)
102	Brian Turner (New Zealand)
101	Dalmar Santos (Brazil)
101	Claudio Taffarel (Brazil)
101	Josef Bozsik (Hungary)

Journeys
Long, Tedious
& Adventurous!

Over the Easter period of 1936, Swansea Town played successive away League games at Plymouth Argyle and Newcastle United in the space of twenty-four hours. The Welsh club beat the Pilgrims 2-1 but lost 2-0 at St James' Park.

Some seventeen years later, Swansea and their supporters travelled north for a third round FA Cup tie at Newcastle in January 1953. A crowd of 63,499 packed into St James' Park to see the game but after just eight minutes' play the referee abandoned proceedings due to fog. Amazingly, over 61,000 fans attended the re-arranged game a few days later, which Newcastle won 3-0.

In January 1927, Plymouth Argyle made an 800-mile round trip to play South Shields in the third round of the FA Cup. This is believed to be the longest journey ever made by a professional club to fulfil a cup tie in this competition without actually leaving England. Unfortunately, it was a wasted trip as the Pilgrims lost 3-1.

Gillingham's 310-mile trip to Barrow in October 1961 took nine-and-a-half hours. They left by coach from the mouth of the Medway River in Kent at 8 a.m., collected a train at Euston Station at 9.05 a.m. and finally arrived at the Holker Street ground at 5.30 p.m. The game kicked off late and was subsequently abandoned in the seventy-fourth minute through poor light with Barrow leading 7-0. The result was allowed to stand. Gillingham set off in good time for their next trip north, to Carlisle, which they won 2-1.

In season 1968/69 Fulham and Preston North End both had wasted overnight 500-mile round-trips to each others' grounds. The Preston match on 2 November was postponed because the Deepdale pitch was waterlogged and the fixture at Craven Cottage on 11 January was called off because seven Fulham players had influenza.

Folkestone made a round-trip of 790 miles to play Stockton in the FA Cup in 1951. They lost 2-1.

League Cup

George 'Stroller' Graham was the first player to appear in four League Cup finals – for Aston Villa in 1961, Chelsea in 1965 and Arsenal in 1968 and 1969.

Aston Villa (1960/61) and West Bromwich Albion (1965/66) both won the League Cup in the first season they entered.

The first all-Midlands League Cup final – and indeed the first all-First Division final – took place in 1963 when Birmingham City beat Aston Villa 3-1 on aggregate.

Liverpool went a record 24 League Cup games without defeat between 1980 and 1983.

Geoff Hurst (West Ham and Stoke City) and Ian Rush (Liverpool and Newcastle United) share the record for scoring the most League Cup goals, with 49.

Longest Match Result

In 1988/89, the longest result ever recorded in world soccer, in terms of letters and figures, came in a third-round Welsh Cup tie which the home side, Kidderminster Harriers, won 3-0 against Llanfairpwllgwyngyllgogerychwyrndrobwllllantysiliogogogoch.

Managers

Sir Alex Ferguson is now regarded as being the most successful manager of all time, having won a total of thirty-four major trophies with Aberdeen and Manchester United. He captured nine with the Dons (three League Championships, four Scottish Cups, one Scottish League Cup and one European Cup-Winners' Cup) and so far has collected twenty-five with United (ten Premiership titles, five FA Cups, two Champions Leagues, a European Cup-Winners' Cup, one Super Cup, two Inter-Continental Cups and two Charity Shields).

Liverpool's Bob Paisley won nineteen prizes during his reign at Anfield: six League titles, three European Cups, three League Cups, one UEFA Cup and six Charity Shields.

Billy Struth was manager at Ibrox Park from August 1920 to April 1953 and during that time Rangers won eighteen Scottish League titles, the Scottish Cup ten times and the League Cup twice. He guided the 'Gers to Scotland's first treble in 1948/49.

Glasgow Rangers had only three official team managers between 1900 and 1966.

Queens Park Rangers' last four managers before the First World War were Englishman Archie Mitchell, Irishman Mick O'Brien, Scotsman Billy Birrell and Welshman Ted Vizard.

Willie Reid managed Norwich City for only five months, during which time they won the 1962 League Cup.

Albert Henderson was caretaker-manager of Arbroath for more than seventeen years, from September 1962 to January 1980.

In April 1986, Jim 'Bald Eagle' Smith became the first man to visit all 92 League grounds in his capacity as a team manager, having done the rounds with Colchester United, Blackburn Rovers, Birmingham City, Oxford United and Queens Park Rangers.

Walsall had ten different managers in eleven years from 1926 to 1937: Joe Burchell, David Ashworth, Jack Torrance, James Kerr, Sid Scholey, Peter O'Rourke, George Saunders (caretaker), Bill Slade, Andy Wilson and Tommy Lowes. The Saddlers had seven during the 1970s, including four in twelve months from 1978 to 1979.

WAYNE

Including caretaker-boss Asa Hartford, Manchester City had five different managers in 1996/97.

Wycombe Wanderers had four managers between October and December 2004.

Four Lancashire clubs – Blackpool, Bolton Wanderers, Blackburn Rovers and Bury – changed managers during the 1970/71 season and all suffered relegation.

Matt Busby, as manager, guided the Great Britain soccer team to fourth place in the 1948 Olympic Games in London. The following year he turned down an offer to become manager of Tottenham Hotspur and also refused the job of manager-coach to the Italian national team.

Hartlepool United FC made ten managerial changes in fourteen years from 1957 to 1971, while West Bromwich Albion made seventeen in twenty-five years from 1975 to 2000. In contrast, West Ham United had only three managers in fifty-nine years up to 1961.

Johnny Cochrane managed both Scottish and FA Cup-winning teams – St Mirren in 1926 and Sunderland in 1937 – the only man to do so before the Second World War. In between times Cochrane managed Reading for just fourteen days from 31 March to 13 April 1929.

In 1959, three of Arsenal's half-backs were Tommy Docherty, Terry Neill and Dave Bowen. Ten years on all three were international team managers, of Scotland, Northern Ireland and Wales respectively.

In eight months – November 1970 to June 1971 inclusive – Bolton Wanderers were managed by four former internationals: Jimmy McIlroy, Jimmy Meadows, Nat Lofthouse and Jimmy Armfield.

West Bromwich Albion had a 'Ron' as manager for ten of the eleven years from 1978 to 1988: Ron Atkinson (two spells), Ronnie Allen, Ron Wylie and Ron Saunders.

Huddersfield Town were managed by Clem Stephenson before the Second World War (from 1929) and his brother George after it (1947-1952).

When he was appointed manager of Carlisle United in August 1946, Ivor Broadis (then aged twenty-three) became the youngest ever manager of a Football League club. He also became the first boss to transfer himself, moving to Sunderland for £18,000 in 1949.

Fred Everiss was secretary-manager of West Bromwich Albion for forty-six years from 1902 to 1948, taking charge of the team throughout the inter-war period. The only other manager to achieve this feat was Bolton's Charles Foweraker.

Billy McCandless guided three Welsh clubs – Cardiff City, Newport County and Swansea Town – to promotion yet never managed an English club.

On 12 February 1994, Fred Davies became the longest-serving caretaker-manager in English League football, having been appointed in May 1993.

Bert Tann, Bill Dodgin and Fred Ford were half-backs with Charlton Athletic in 1936/37. In the 1960s all three had spells as manager of Bristol Rovers.

Sunderland did not have an Englishman as manager until Allan Brown took over in 1957. In the previous sixty-nine years there had been five Scots and an Irishman in charge of team affairs.

Herbert Chapman was the first manager to guide two different teams – Huddersfield Town and Arsenal – to the Football League Championship.

Fifteen players who won full England caps during the 1948/49 season went on to become Football League club managers. They were Roy Bentley, Henry Cockburn, Jimmy Dickinson, Neil Franklin, Jimmy Hagan, Tommy Lawton, Jackie Milburn, Stanley Matthews, Stan Mortensen, Stan Pearson, Alf Ramsey, Jack Rowley, Laurie Scott, Tim Ward and Billy Wright.

Jock Rutherford retired as an Arsenal player in March 1923 to take over as manager of Stoke. He quit the position after just six months and rejoined the Gunners as a player.

Alf Ramsey received a £6,000 bonus – plus a knighthood – when he guided England to World Cup glory in 1966. The twenty-two players in his squad each collected a £1,000 victory award.

David Steele managed two clubs at the same time – Bradford Park Avenue and Huddersfield Town in September 1943.

Luton Town did not have a manager when they reached the FA Cup final in 1959.

Bill Nicholson's first game in charge of Spurs resulted in a handsome win when Everton were thrashed 10-4 in a League game at White Hart Lane in October 1958.

Andy Beattie was the first man to manage as many as eight different League clubs. He was also Scotland's first full-time manager, appointed in 1954. Beattie in fact managed clubs in three different divisions in the space of three months in 1951/52: Stockport County in the Third Division (North), Huddersfield Town in the First Division and the same club in the Second Division after suffering relegation.

Steve Murray was manager of Falkirk for just seventy-two hours during mid-August 1980.

Bobby Williamson's first game in charge of Plymouth Argyle coincided with the Pilgrims beating QPR to clinch promotion from the Second Division to the First on 24 April 2004.

Dave Bassett was appointed manager of Crystal Palace in May 1984 but walked out of Selhurst Park twenty-four hours later, not having signed a contract.

Four post-Second World War managers of Workington played for Bradford clubs – Sam Barkas and Joe Harvey for City, Albert Flatley and George Ainsley for Park Avenue.

Tim Ward was manager of Exeter City for only a week in March 1953 while former Northern Ireland international Jimmy McIlroy was in charge of Bolton Wanderers for just sixteen days during November 1970.

Frank Gardner was elected manager-secretary of Leicester Fosse in 1884 at the age of eighteen, making him possibly the youngest manager in football history.

Don Revie achieved several 'firsts' during his managerial career at Leeds United. He was the first boss to take a club side to Wembley on four occasions; saw his side become the first British team to win the Fairs Cup in 1968 and became the first manager to claim that same trophy twice when they won it again in 1971.

As players, Revie (with Manchester City) and Bob Stokoe (with Newcastle United) were on opposing sides as players in the 1955 FA Cup final. Eighteen years later the same two men, then of Leeds and Sunderland respectively, were the managers at the 1973 cup final.

As a manager in the 1940s and '50s, Harry Storer signed Martin O'Donnell for Coventry City, Birmingham City and Derby County. Arthur Turner did something similar in the 1950s when he recruited Bill Finney for Crewe Alexandra, Stoke and Birmingham City.

Alec Stock was player-manager of FA Cup giant-killers Yeovil in 1949; he managed Leyton Orient when they won the Third Division (South) title in 1956; he was in charge of Queens Park Rangers when they completed the League Cup and Third Division Championship double in 1967 and finished runners-up in the Second Division a year later; he took Luton Town into the Second Division in 1970 and led Fulham to the FA Cup final in 1975.

Between 1957 and 1964 Archie Macaulay managed in all four divisions of the Football League: at Norwich City in the Second and Third Divisions, at West Bromwich Albion in the First Division and at Brighton & Hove Albion in the Third and Fourth Divisions.

Matches

Football League/Premiership

Arsenal hold the record for playing most Premiership home games without defeat – 32 from May 2003 to January 2005. The Gunners also hold the record for most away games without defeat – 27 – achieved over a period of eighteen months between April 2003 and October 2004. Chelsea were near to breaking that record in September 2005.

Sunderland celebrated their 2,000th home League match by beating neighbours Middlesbrough 1-0 at the Stadium of Light in December 2000.

The First Division game between The Wednesday and Aston Villa on 26 November 1898 was abandoned with just over 10 minutes remaining. At the time Wednesday

were leading 3-1 but the Football League would not let the score stand and ordered the teams to return in March to play out the last few minutes. In that time the Owls scored again to win the game 4-1.

Sunderland were undefeated in 44 home League games between September 1890 and December 1893. In 1890/91 they won all 13 home matches.

Millwall went 59 home League games without defeat from August 1964 to January 1967. Plymouth Argyle ended that run. Millwall also went 19 Fourth Division games without defeat at the start of the 1959/60 season.

In April 1933, Reading commenced an unbeaten home League run of 55 games. It ended in January 1936 when QPR won 2-1.

In October 1985, Reading broke Tottenham Hotspur's record of 11 successive League wins at the start of a season when they defeated Newport County 2-0.

Liverpool played fifteen League games in London between March 1972 and October 1974 and did not lose a single one. Earlier, in 1934/35, they made just three trips to the capital and lost each time: 8-1 at Arsenal, 4-1 at Chelsea and 5-1 at Tottenham.

Swindon Town's first ever League game, against Swansea Town in August 1920, resulted in a 9-1 win.

On 11 March 1939, Everton and Liverpool both drew their respective League games against Middlesbrough and Portsmouth 4-4.

Tottenham Hotspur won their opening eleven League games at the start of the 1960/61 season and, by carrying two over from the previous campaign, actually recorded 13 successive wins in the First Division.

Over a period of four years from 1959 to 1963, 8 Second Division games involving Charlton Athletic and Plymouth Argyle produced 60 goals: The results were:

1959/60	Charlton 5-2 Plymouth	Plymouth 6-4 Charlton
1960/61	Charlton 6-4 Plymouth	Plymouth 6-4 Charlton
1961/62	Charlton 3-1 Plymouth	Plymouth 2-1 Charlton
1962/63	Charlton 6-3 Plymouth	Plymouth 6-1 Charlton

Cup Action

Blackpool were the first team to win the FA Cup after being two goals down. In 1953 they came back to beat Bolton 4-3 in what was has become known as the Matthews Final.

The second leg of the Football League Wartime Cup tie between Cardiff City and Bristol City in April 1945 lasted for exactly 200 minutes – the kick-off was at 3 p.m. and the final whistle sounded at 6.40 p.m.

The following year, in March 1946, the Stockport County v. Doncaster Rovers Third Division (North) Cup tie lasted for 203 minutes. Kick-off was at 3.30 p.m. but, owing to the poor light, play was continuously halted by the referee who believed the conditions would improve. They did – and he eventually blew the final whistle at 7.03 that evening.

Over a period of twenty-one years, from May 1965 to May 1986, Liverpool took part in twenty-three major cup finals, including replays. They won thirteen, including a penalty shoot-out decider, drew four and lost six. They also took part in two European Super Cup finals (four games in total) and two World Club Championship matches.

Leeds United competed in fourteen major cup finals in eleven seasons from 1964/65 to 1975/76. They won three, drew five and lost six. Norman Hunter played in all of them.

Manchester City and Leicester City met four times in successive seasons in the FA Cup, the last occasion, in 1969, saw the Mancunians win the trophy at Wembley with a 1-0 victory.

In successive years, in January 1955, 1956 and 1957, Leeds United met Cardiff City at Elland Road in the third round of the FA Cup. Each time Cardiff won 2-1.

Fulham played twenty cup matches in 2002/03, participating in the Intertoto, UEFA, League and FA Cup competitions.

The Scottish Game

Celtic defeated Raith Rovers 6-0 and Motherwell 3-1 on the same day in April 1916.

On 9 February 1963, the whole of the Scottish League programme was wiped out because of snow and ice.

Celtic had an unbeaten League run of 63 games from November 1915 to April 1917.

After losing the 1966 Scottish Cup final, Celtic went 33 games without defeat.

During the twelve-month period from March 1928 to March 1929 Rangers went 38 games unbeaten in the Scottish First Division.

Overseas Football

A non-competitive match in Buenos Aires in November 1951 lasted for twelve hours ten minutes – it was arranged as a mark of respect for the President of the Argentine and his wife.

The Western Hemisphere Club Championship game between Santos (Brazil) and Penarol (Uruguay) in 1962 lasted for three hours thirty-three minutes, covering two days. It started at 9.30 p.m. on 2 August and finished in the early hours of the following morning. It ended level at 3-3.

In 1950 a team of fat men weighing a total of 1.5 tons beat a thin team weighing half a ton by three goals to two in Bilbao, Spain.

The final result of a Swiss League game was Chiasso 0 Young Boys of Berne 8. The corner-kick count was Chiasso 13 Young Boys of Berne 0.

Real Madrid were undefeated at home in 122 League and cup games from 3 February 1957 to 7 May 1965. They won 114 and drew 8. Atletico Madrid ended that run with a 1-0 defeat.

Hungary played 29 internationals without defeat between May 1950 and the World Cup final in July 1954.

General Club Facts

Liverpool went 85 home games without defeat between January 1978 and January 1981 – a record. Their total comprised 63 League, 9 League Cup, 7 European, and 6 FA Cup matches.

Stockport County went 51 home games without defeat (48 League, 3 FA Cup) between April 1927 and October 1929.

Sunderland were undefeated in 44 home games between September 1890 and December 1893. They followed this soon afterwards with another 37-match unbeaten home run up to September 1896. In all they suffered 1 defeat in 82 home matches covering a period of six years.

In season 1971/72, Tottenham Hotspur fulfilled a record 68 competitive games: 42 in the League, 5 in the FA Cup, 7 in the League Cup, 2 in the Anglo-Italian Cup and 12 in the UEFA Cup, which they won. Peterborough United played 67 in 1991/92.

In season 1969/70 Leeds United played ten First Division matches against London teams and didn't lose any of them, winning five and drawing five. They also drew 2-2 with Chelsea in the FA Cup final but lost the replay 2-1.

In 1887/88, the season before the foundation of the Football League, Preston North End went 43 games without defeat. The run ended when they lost 2-1 to West Bromwich Albion in the FA Cup final.

Middlesbrough played 8 out of 9 League and cup games at home between 20 November 1926 and 15 January 1927. They won 6 and drew 2, and scored 32 goals.

In contrast, Coventry City played eight successive away games – seven in the League, one in the FA Cup – between January and April 1977. Swindon Town played six Fourth Division games on the trot away from home during 1986 and won them all.

Everton and Sunderland met four times in five weeks in 1933/34 (two League and three FA Cup games).

Over a period of seven-and-a-half weeks from 4 March 1911 to 29 April 1911, Stoke played 19 matches. They used 24 players of which only two were ever-present.

Between October 1984 and September 1985, Everton and Manchester United met in five different competitions: the Football League, the FA Cup, League Cup, FA Charity Shield and Screen Sports Super Cup.

Liverpool lost twenty-two successive away League and cup games over the course of a year from February 1953 to February 1954.

Medal Winners

Full-back Jim Welford collected English, Scottish and Irish FA Cup medals with Aston Villa (1895 cup-winners), Celtic (1899 cup-winners) and Belfast Celtic (1906 runners-up) respectively.

Right-winger Jimmy Delaney also achieved a triple feat, gaining Cup winners' medals with Celtic in 1937, Manchester United in 1948 and Derry City in 1954.

In fact, Delaney won a fourth cup medal in 1956 when Cork Athletic finished runners-up in the FAI Cup final. He also claimed two League Championships with Celtic in 1936 and 1938.

Forward Jim Bone received two winners' medals in the same season with different clubs. In 1971/72 he helped Partick Thistle win the Scottish League Cup and later was a key member of Norwich City's Second Division Championship winning side.

Before he was twenty years of age, Arsenal's Devon-born left-winger Cliff Bastin (once of Exeter City) had gained League Championship, FA Cup and FA Charity Shield winners' medals and a full England cap.

Between 1904 and 1921, Jimmy 'Napoleon' McMenemy won seven Scottish Cup medals, six with Celtic, one with Partick Thistle.

In 1951, Bill Slater collected an FA Cup runners-up medal as an amateur with Blackpool and nine years later, as captain, gained a winners' medal in the same competition as a professional with Wolves.

Dutchman Arie Haan won European Cup winners' medals in 1971, 1972 and 1973 and European Cup-Winners' Cup medals in 1976 and 1978.

Full-back Bobby Cowell, winger Bobby Mitchell and centre forward Jackie Milburn all gained three FA Cup winners' medals with Newcastle in 1951, 1952 and 1955. The trio appeared in all twenty-five Cup ties played by the Geordies in those seasons.

Joe Smith was a player with Bolton Wanderers when they won the FA Cup in 1923 and 1926. He later managed Blackpool in three FA Cup finals, 1948, 1951 and 1953, collecting his third winners' medal in the lattermost.

The Liverpool duo of Alan Hansen (1979-1990) and Phil Neal (1976-1986) each gained eight League Championship winners' medals with the Merseysiders. Ryan Giggs has so far won ten Premiership medals with Manchester United.

Arsenal left-back Gael Clichy is believed to be the youngest player (aged 20) to win a Premiership championship medal, doing so in 2005.

Paul Terry (Barnet) and his brother John (Chelsea) won Championship medals with their respective clubs in 2004–05.

Name Game

The footballer with the longest name ever to appear in a League game is Arthur Griffith Stanley Sackville Redvers Trevor Boscawen Trevis who lined up at centre half for West Bromwich Albion against Liverpool in April 1934, his only senior outing for the Midlands club.

In 1931/32, Cardiff City had four 'Macs' on their books, each coming from a different country. They were McGrath (England), McNally (Scotland), McJennett (Wales) and McCambridge (Ireland).

In the 1930s, West Bromwich Albion had two players named William Richardson. To make it easy for them to be identified the centre forward was called 'W.G.' while his colleague and centre half was referred to as Bill.

In the mid-1950s, Barnsley's defence included players named Short, Sharp and Swift while Huddersfield had players named Goy, Hoy and Joy in their ranks in the 1960s.

Lightning FC of Brazzaville, Republic of the Congo, decided to change their name to Hurricane FC after playing a series of games in high winds!

In 1965, Preston North End had a winger named Ray Veall. Five years later they signed Bobby Ham, an inside forward. Some years earlier, in the 1920s, a player named Arthur Bacon had an unsuccessful trial at Deepdale.

In 1980, Trevor Cherry of Leeds United was booked for fouling Steve Grapes of Norwich City.

In 1950/51 Rotherham United fielded four players named Williams who were unrelated: Horace, Bobby, Danny and Ken.

Charles Faultless was a 1950s Scottish League referee.

Nicknames

In the 1920s, Aston Villa's half-back trio of Jimmy Gibson, Alec Talbot and Joe Tate were respectively nicknamed 'Wind, Sleet and Rain'.

In the 1930s the middle three in the first team of neighbours West Bromwich Albion – Jack Sankey, Bill Richardson and Jimmy Edwards – were nicknamed 'Salt, Pepper and Mustard'.

Jim Hammond, who played for Fulham between 1929 and 1938, was called the 'Galloping Hairpin'.

Jimmy 'Betty Grable Legs' Elder played for Colchester United and Portsmouth between 1945 and 1955.

Jackie Smith, a 1930s forward with Barnsley, was nicknamed 'Tiny' and 'Peter Pan' because of his 5ft 3in height.

Fred 'Carnera' Gibbons scored a hat-trick from the centre half position for Fulham in a League game against Southampton at Craven Cottage in November 1934.

The 1930s West Bromwich Albion full-back George Shaw was named 'Teapot' because he was always filling the cups up in the dressing room.

Jim Towers and George Francis were Brentford's 'Terrible Twins' in the 1950s. They scored 153 and 124 League goals respectively for the club.

Also in the 1950s, the West Bromwich Albion strike-force of Ronnie Allen and Johnny Nicholls were also known as the 'Terrible Twins', with Nicholls also being called 'Poacher' and 'Johnny on the Spot'.

Tom 'Pongo' Waring was a champion goalscorer for Aston Villa in the 1930s and before him the Midland club had a centre forward nicknamed 'Appy Arry' Hampton, the 'Wellington Whirlwind' while Everton's star striker was Ralph 'Dixie' Dean.

There has been 'Gentleman' Jim Baxter (Rangers and Scotland), 'Gentleman' Jim Howie (Bristol Rovers) and 'Gentleman' 'Jem' Bayliss (West Bromwich Albion), as well as 'Big Jim' Bowie (Oldham Athletic). Bayliss' nickname 'Jem' was taken from the initials of three of his four Christian names: James Edward Matthias.

Willie 'Demon' Devlin scored 15 goals in 19 games for Liverpool in the 1920s.

Joe 'Bubbles' Bailey, an England amateur international, scored Reading's first League goal, against Newport County in August 1920. He won the DSO, MC and Bar in the First World War.

Fred 'Spider' Parker played for Clapton Orient and joined the Footballers' Battalion during the First World War.

Frank 'Swerver' Richardson scored four goals when Swindon Town came from 2-0 down to beat Bournemouth 8-2 in January 1926.

Hungary's great side of the 1950s, which crushed England 6-3 at Wembley in 1953 and 7-1 in Budapest in 1954, were called the 'Marvellous Magyars' with star player Ferenc Puskas nicknamed the 'Galloping Major.'

After beating England 5-1 in London in 1928, Scotland's eleven players were dubbed 'The Wembley Wizards.'

Several other players had nicknames: Allan 'Sniffer' Clarke, Tony 'Bomber' Brown, Norman 'Bites your legs' Hunter and David 'Golden balls' Beckham.

There have also been the Busby Babes (Manchester United) and Mercer's Minnows (Aston Villa).

Non-League

Between 1948 and 1965, Halifax Town played six FA Cup ties at home against non-League opposition and failed to win any, losing in turn to Scunthorpe United, Ashington, Ashton United, Rhyl Athletic, Burton Albion and South Liverpool.

Exeter City, of the Nationwide Conference, held mighty Manchester United to a 0-0 draw in front of more than 67,000 fans at Old Trafford in a third-round FA Cup tie in January 2005. The replay ended Exeter 0 United 2 – attendance 9,033.

Own Goals

Sam Wynne scored twice for both sides in a League game in October 1923, netting with a free-kick and a penalty for his own club Oldham Athletic and knocking in two own goals for the opposition, Manchester United.

Aston Villa centre half Chris Nicholl also scored two own goals when playing against Leicester City in March 1976 but made amends by netting twice for his own side in a 2-2 draw.

When Carlisle United beat Rochdale 7-2 in a League game on Christmas Day 1954, three of their goals were scored by Rochdale players: George Underwood, Harry Boyle and Danny Murphy.

Everton full-back Tommy Wright scored own goals on successive Saturdays in March 1972, within thirty-three and thirty-two seconds of the kick-off against Liverpool and Manchester City respectively.

Between 1956 and 1962, defender Danny Malloy of Cardiff City scored what is probably a record number of own goals, a total of 14.

In season 1934/35 Middlesbrough defender Bob Stuart conceded 4 own goals – a Football League record.

Alan Hopper of Barnsley scored 4 own goals in 5 games in the 1960s, while the West Bromwich Albion centre half Stan Jones registered 4 in 12 outings in the same decade.

In 1968/69 Jose Ramirez, right full-back of Argentina's FC Cafuento, scored a hat-trick in fifty-five minutes against Perosa. Just one thing wrong, they were all own goals. Ramirez was later switched to centre forward!

Den Haag players conceded three own goals in their UEFA Cup game against Wolves at Molineux in 1971/72. Wolves won 4-0 for a 7-1 aggregate victory.

In February 1950, a Scottish Cup tie between Clyde and Raith Rovers ended in a 3-2 win for Rovers, whose goals were all scored by Clyde players: Frank Mennie with two and Bob Milligan were the men responsible.

On 17 December 1955, as Arsenal led Blackpool at Highbury, an excited spectator in the crowd sounded a whistle. Full-back Dennis Evans, thinking it was referee Frank Coultas blowing for full time, celebrated a 4-0 win by banging the ball into his own net. Twenty seconds later, full time was called with the Gunners 4-1 winners.

With both teams already assured of a place in the semi-finals of the 1998 Tiger5 Cup competition, Thailand played Indonesia, knowing that the winners would face the dreaded task of facing the host nation Vietnam. Neither wanted that fixture. After a dull first half, which ended goal-less, the teams did better after the break and with a minute remaining the scores were level at 2-2. Then, out of the blue, the Indonesian defender Mursyid Effendi hammered the ball past his own 'keeper to give Thailand victory. As expected, Thailand lost 3-0 to Vietnam while Indonesia also lost, going down 2-1 to Singapore. Both federations were fined £25,000 and banned.

Jonathan Woodgate scored a superb own goal when making his debut for Real Madrid against Athletic Bilbao in September 2005 – and was later sent off. He had waited fifty-six weeks for his first start for the Spaniards.

WAYNE

Penalties

League Competitions

The first player to successfully score from the penalty spot was Joe Heath for Wolves in a Football League game against Accrington in September 1891. It is on record that the first penalty in Scotland was scored in January 1891.

The fastest penalty ever awarded – and indeed scored – came after just ten seconds of the Torquay United *v.* Walsall Third Division (South) game in August 1956. Sammy Collins of Torquay was the successful taker.

Johann Neeskens scored a first-minute penalty for Holland against West Germany in the 1974 World Cup final in Munich, awarded by English referee Jack Taylor. Taylor later gave the Germans a spot-kick, which was also converted.

Bolton goalkeeper Juusi Jaaskelainen saved two penalties in the last three minutes to earn his side a 1–0 home Premiership win over Blackburn Rovers in 2006.

Francis Lee converted a record 13 penalties in 1971/72 for Manchester City. Eleven spot-kicks were scored by Jack Ball (Sheffield Wednesday) by Willie Hall

(Tottenham Hotspur) in season 1932/33 and by Andy Johnson (Crystal Palace) in 2004/05.

On the very last day of the 1980/81 Second Division programme, Don Givens of Sheffield United missed a penalty against Walsall with the final kick of the game. As a result the Blades were relegated and the Saddlers, who won 1-0, stayed up.

Burnley players missed three penalties (all saved by 'keeper Billy Scott) and converted one (Abbott hitting the net) during a League game against Grimsby Town in February 1909. The Clarets won 2-0.

Five penalties were awarded in the Second Division game between Crystal Palace and Brighton & Hove Albion in 1988/89. Each side scored once but Palace missed another three.

There were also five spot-kicks awarded in the World Cup game between Mexico and Argentina in Montevideo in 1930. Argentina won 6-3.

George Dick scored twice from the penalty spot in fifty-five seconds for Stockport County against Shrewsbury Town in January 1951.

Manchester City players missed three penalties in a League game against Newcastle United in January 1912. The result was 1-1.

Rotherham United goalkeeper Herbert Emery saved 9 out of 10 penalties in first- and second-team football in 1929/30.

Top-scorer for Southend in 1921/22 was full-back Jimmy Evans, who scored 10 goals from penalties.

Birmingham City debutant goalkeeper Tony Coton saved a penalty with his first touch of the ball against Sunderland in December 1980.

In April 2001, Phil Wilson did the same thing for Oxford United against Bristol Rovers and likewise Joe Murphy for West Bromwich Albion from Liverpool's Michael Owen at Anfield in September 2002.

When Matt Le Tissier scored his 48th penalty out of an eventual 49 for Southampton on 1 April 2000 against Sunderland, it was also his 100th goal in the Premiership.

Willie Cook of Everton scored three penalties in separate matches in the space of just four days, 24-27 December 1938.

Manchester City missed a penalty in their final League game of the 1925/26 season against Newcastle United and as a result were relegated to the Second Division.

Portsmouth striker Yakubu was asked to take the same penalty kick three times during a home Premiership game with Norwich City in January 2005. He scored each time in his side's 1-1 draw.

In their final League match of the 1923/24 season a missed penalty at Birmingham cost Cardiff City the First Division Championship; they finished runners-up behind Huddersfield Town on goal average.

Four penalties were awarded in the space of five minutes during the League game between Crewe Alexandra and Bradford Park Avenue in March 1924.

Both goalkeepers – John Brownlie of Third Lanark and Charlie Hampton of Motherwell – converted penalty kicks during a Scottish First Division game in 1910.

Plymouth 'keeper Fred Craig tucked away five penalties in the late 1920s, while Chesterfield's goalkeeper Arnold Birch got the same number in a single season, netting five times from the spot in the 1923/24 campaign.

Southampton right-back Tom Parker missed a penalty against Northampton Town in a Southern League fixture in October 1919. Later in the game he went in goal and saved a spot-kick. The Cobblers still won 6-2 at The Dell.

Six times the Partick Thistle goalkeeper saved a spot-kick against Kilmarnock in October 1945, and each time the referee ordered it to be retaken because he judged the 'keeper to have moved. A seventh save was made and this time the referee ruled it legitimate.

Over a period of four years, 19 penalties were awarded to Bradford Park Avenue in Third Division (North) matches. Amazingly 16 were missed.

Southend United players missed seven successive penalties during 1991.

Wolves' full-back Geoff Palmer scored a penalty against Liverpool after just fifty-five seconds of the opening League game of 1982/83. It was his only goal that season.

Sheffield Wednesday were not awarded a penalty in 82 matches between December 1964 and October 1986.

Earlier, in a League game at Preston in August 1953, the Sheffield Wednesday defender Norman Curtis went in goal and saved two penalties, one taken by Tom Finney. The Owls still lost 6-0.

Harry Potts of Burnley missed three penalties in successive games in the space of ten days in January 1948.

Stan Lynn netted from the penalty spot in five successive League games for

Birmingham City, against Liverpool and Sheffield United in the last two fixtures of 1963/64 and against Nottingham Forest, Fulham and Stoke City in the first three games of 1964/65. He ended the latter season with eight successful penalty conversions to his name.

John Collins of Cambridge United netted from the spot in four consecutive League games during September and October 1972.

Robbie Fowler's late penalty miss for Manchester City v. Middlesbrough on the final day of the 2004/05 Premiership programme cost his side a place in the UEFA Cup.

Cup Spot-kicks

West Bromwich Albion centre forward Ronnie Allen scored penalties in both the semi-final and final of the 1953/54 FA Cup competition, the first against his former club Port Vale, the second against Preston North End at Wembley.

Five penalties were awarded in the Ipswich Town v. Lowestoft Town FA Cup tie in October 1936. Ipswich scored three while Lowestoft scored one and missed one. Ipswich won the game 7-1.

Eddie Shimwell of Blackpool was the first full-back to score a penalty in a Wembley FA Cup final, doing so against Manchester United in 1948.

In 1988, John Aldridge of Liverpool saw his penalty saved by Wimbledon goalkeeper Dave Beasant – the first time a player failed to convert a spot-kick in a Wembley FA Cup final.

The first penalty scored in an FA Cup final was by Albert Shepherd for Newcastle United against Barnsley in 1910.

The first player to miss a penalty in an FA Cup final was Charlie Wallace of Aston Villa against Sunderland in 1913. Villa still won 1-0.

Hat-tricks of Penalties

The first player to score a hat-trick of penalties was Billy Walker for Aston Villa against Bradford City in a League Division One game in November 1921.

Full-back George Milburn put away a hat-trick of spot-kicks in the space of twenty-one second-half minutes to earn his side, Chesterfield, a 4-2 win over Sheffield Wednesday in a League game in June 1947.

Alan Slough scored a hat-trick of penalties for Peterborough United at Chester in April 1978, but Posh still lost 4-3.

Overseas/European

Josif Sabo, who played for Dynamo Kiev, Czernomorec Odessa and Dynamo Moscow, never missed a penalty in his professional career (1959-1972). He had a 100 percent record with 73 successful spot-kick conversions in more than 350 club matches and 35 internationals for Russia – a lot of games considering that he missed more than 100 through suspensions and injury.

German player Frank Ordenewicz was presented with the FIFA Fair Play Award for 1988 after persuading the referee to award a penalty against his own team in a Bundesliga match.

Internationals

Five penalties were awarded during the 1930 World Cup game between Argentina and Mexico in Uruguay.

England U21s lost 13–12 in a penalty shoot-out against Holland in 2006–07.

General

The former Birmingham City, Ipswich Town, Leicester City, Manchester City and Stockport County 'keeper Paul Cooper saved over 25 spot-kicks between 1971 and 1991, likewise Jimmy Sanders (West Bromwich Albion and Coventry City) between 1945 and 1959.

In 1959/60 Crystal Palace full-back Alf Noakes scored 4 penalties, missed another 3, netted a goal from open play and was credited with an own goal, all in the space of 11 matches.

In season 1954/55 Liverpool were awarded 10 penalties in 8 games. One was saved but the other 9 resulted in goals.

Eric Houghton scored 79 out of 86 penalties at various levels for Aston Villa. He missed his first, in the fifth minute of his debut against Leeds United in 1930, but scored his last, against Huddersfield Town reserves in 1946. Houghton also scored from the spot for England.

Players

Football League & Clubs

In 1973 four players with the name of Best were registered with Football League clubs and each was born in a different country. They were Ipswich Town's David (England), Manchester United's George (Northern Ireland), West Ham's Clyde (Bermuda) and Northampton Town's Billy (Scotland).

The surnames of thirteen West Ham United players during the mid-1960s began with the letter 'B': Jim Barrett, John Bond, Jack Burkitt, Eddie Bovington, Ronnie Boyce, Ken Brown, Peter Brabrook, Johnny Byrne, David Bickles, Peter Bennett, Martin Britt, Dennis Burnett and Ray Bloomfield.

Cyrille Regis played League football for West Midlands clubs West Bromwich Albion, Coventry City, Aston Villa and Wolves in the 1980s and 1990s – the first player ever to do so at professional level.

During the 1997/98 season, Steve Palmer wore fourteen different numbered shirts when Watford won the Second Division Championship. He started the last game of the season in goal wearing number one before switching with regular 'keeper Alex Chamberlain after just five seconds.

Stenhousemuir used a total of forty-five players during the 1986/87 League season (seven were goalkeepers) while Stirling Albion called up at total of fifty players in 1963/64 when they finished bottom of the Second Division in Scotland. The following season they won the championship.

Full-back Alf Ramsey helped Tottenham Hotspur win both the Second and First Division Championships as a player in 1950 and 1951. He then repeated that feat as a manager with Ipswich Town in 1961 and 1962. Four years later he won the World Cup as England boss.

Brentford fielded an unchanged team in twenty consecutive Third Division (South) matches between 2 November 1929 and 15 March 1930 – a Football League record at that time. The same season the Bees created another record by winning all their 21 home League games.

Centre forward Frank Neary played League football for five different London clubs: Fulham, Queens Park Rangers (two spells), West Ham United, Leyton Orient and Millwall. He was top-scorer for Orient in successive seasons: 1947/48 and 1948/49.

Tranmere Rovers were unchanged for the first twenty-eight League games of the 1977/78 season. Liverpool were unchanged for the first twelve in the First Division in 1967/68 and made only one change in the first seventeen fixtures.

Norwich City fielded an unchanged team for the first twenty-three League games of their 1950/51 League programme.

Top-line striker David Halliday scored four goals for Arsenal in a 6-6 League encounter with Leicester City just five days before the 1930 FA Cup final but was then left out of the side to face Huddersfield Town when Jack Lambert reported fit after injury.

Jimmy Thompson, who played League football for Hearts, Portsmouth, Coventry City and Bury between 1904-1919 and later managed Bury, Swansea Town and Halifax Town, hailed from a more northerly point of the British Isles than any other player in the game's history. He was born in the Shetland Isles in 1884.

Walsall fielded only eight players – seven regulars and a committee member – when losing 12-0 in a League game at Darwen on Boxing Day 1896.

West Bromwich Albion tried seven different players in the centre forward position during the 1904/05 season.

Liverpool and Aston Villa used only fourteen players in 42 games when they won the League title in 1965/66 and 1980/81 respectively.

Owing to atrocious weather conditions, Chelsea finished their League game with Blackpool in October 1932 with only six players on the pitch.

Q: When did Charlton score for Charlton when Charlton didn't score themselves?
A: In April 1957 when Arsenal's full-back Stan Charlton scored an own-goal in his side's 3-1 League win at Highbury, which drove another nail into the Addicks' relegation coffin.

Over a period of twenty years, from 1927 to 1946 inclusive, Arsenal featured five doctors in League games, all of them forwards: James Paterson, James Marshall, George Little, Kevin O'Flanagan and Alec Cross.

On 26 August 1933, the five players of whom Walsall's forward line against York City was comprised in a Third Division (North) game had all previously served with Coventry City: Woolhouse, Ball, Alsop, Sheppard and Lee.

During the 1923/24 season Jack Byers set a unique record by playing in four First Division matches against both Chelsea and Newcastle United for Blackburn Rovers and West Bromwich Albion in turn.

The Reverend Kenneth Hunt, a right half, and the Reverend Billy Jordan, a centre forward, turned out for Wolves in 1912/13 – the only case in League football history of two parsons playing together in the same side. Hunt also scored for Wolves when they won the FA Cup in 1908.

James Oakes is almost certainly the only man to play for both sides in the same Football League match. On Boxing Day 1932 he turned out for Charlton Athletic against Port Vale but the referee abandoned proceedings early in the second half. By the time the game was replayed Oakes had become a Vale player, and he duly lined up for his new club against his old one.

Arsenal beat Crystal Palace 5–1 in 2005 without an English-born player in their line-up.

Cup Competitions

Clem Stephenson played in four FA Cup finals at three venues and later managed teams in two other finals. He was in two victorious Aston Villa teams that won the trophy in 1913 at Crystal Palace and 1920 at Stamford Bridge and was also a member of the triumphant Huddersfield Town side of 1922, also at Stamford Bridge, having been on the Terriers' losing side of 1928 at Wembley. As a manager, he saw Huddersfield lose both the 1930 and 1938 finals.

West Bromwich Albion have twice fielded an all-English XI when winning the FA Cup, first in 1888 against Preston North End and again in 1931 against Birmingham.

There was not one single international player in Sunderland's FA Cup-winning team that beat Leeds United in 1973.

Frank Saul was the only uncapped player in Tottenham's 1967 FA Cup-winning side.

On 20 October 1998, Aston Villa's team for their UEFA Cup second round first leg clash with Celta Vigo consisted entirely of English-born players. Villa won 1-0.

Foreign Connection

Arsenal set a record by starting their Champions League game against Hamburg in 2006 with 11 different players from 11 different countries.

Middlesbrough became the first British club to field three Brazilian players when Juninho, Emerson and Branco appeared in a 7-0 home win against Hereford United in a League Cup tie in September 1996.

Charlton Athletic manager Jimmy Seed signed thirteen South African players between December 1946 and September 1956. Four became household names at The Valley: Eddie Firmani, Sid O'Linn, Stuart Leary and John Hewie, who formed part of Athletic's team in 1953/54 along with Ken Chamberlain. Surprisingly, Hewie went on to play for Scotland.

In the early 1960s, players of the unsuccessful Paelem club from Belgium vowed not to shave until they won a game – it took them 35 matches before they used a razor!

Lucien Emile Boullimier was a Stoke wing half in 1896/97. He was also an accomplished musician, opera singer, artist and actor. He was the son of the world famous Parisien ceramic artist Anton Boullimier.

In the early 1960s Tore Hansen of Fredrikstad in Norway, aged fifteen, set a world record of keeping the ball in the air for two hours twenty-one minutes. Watched by four referees, he headed, kicked and bounced the ball off his body no less than 16,098 times without it ever touching the ground.

On the afternoon of 11 November 1987, Mark Hughes played for Wales against Czechoslovakia. In the evening he starred for Bayern Munich against Manchester United.

Short and the Tall

One of the tallest players ever to appear in a Football League game is Bill Carr, goalkeeper for Bournemouth, who measured 6ft 9ins in 1924.

Striker Kevin Francis, who played for Derby County, Birmingham City, Stockport County and Hull City between 1979 and 2001, stood 6ft 7ins tall, as does Peter Crouch of Liverpool, while Fulham defender Zat Knight is 6ft 6ins.

One of the smallest players has been Grimsby Town's 1930s star Jackie Bestall at 5ft 2ins. Tommy Magee of West Bromwich Albion stood a fraction over 5ft 2ins while Freddie le May of Watford and Clapton Orient was around 5ft 3ins. Barnsley's 1930s forward Jackie Smith and 'Fanny' Walden of Spurs were also 5ft 3ins tall and weighed barely 9st 4lbs, while another Barnsley player, Walter Hepworth, at 5ft 4ins, tipped the scales at 7st 5lbs during the 1890s.

Tottenham Hotspur fielded what is believed to have been probably the smallest and lightest pair of wingers ever seen in a Football League team when they played West Bromwich Albion on 21 October 1922. 'Fanny' Walden (mentioned above) was at outside right while on the opposite flank was Sammy Brookes, who was 5ft 4ins tall and weighed just nine stones.

In the late 1950s Lincoln City's centre forward was 6ft 1in Ray Long, while their left-winger was 'Joey' Short, who was 5ft 4ins tall.

Player Facts

In 1977, George Best played football in four different countries in ten days: for Fulham against Crystal Palace in England and against Cardiff City in Wales; for Northern Ireland against Iceland in Belfast and in a friendly for Fulham against St Johnstone in Scotland.

Con Martin made 213 League appearances for Aston Villa between 1948 and 1956. Of these, 176 were at centre half, 8 at right-back, 8 at left-back and 27 in goal.

Right-backs Fred Furniss of Sheffield United – with two penalties – and Ernie Devlin of West Ham United – with two own goals – contributed two goals each in a League game at Upton Park in September 1950. The Blades won 5-3 despite Bill Robinson's hat-trick for the Hammers.

Norman Wood, playing for Stockport County against Fulham on 4 October 1913, headed into his own goal, handled to conceded a penalty, which was converted, and then failed with a spot-kick himself, all in the space of thirteen minutes. Fulham won 3-1.

In 1910, Dai Davies, a goalkeeper with Bolton Wanderers from 1902 to 1910 and a forward for rugby league clubs Swinton (1898-1902 and 1910-1913) and Leigh (1913-1914) became the only man in history to win caps at full international level for Wales in both codes of football. He played soccer against Scotland and Ireland in 1904 and England in 1908 and lined up against England at rugby in 1910. He also won a Rugby League Challenge Cup medal in 1900 and played for Bolton in the 1904 FA Cup final.

Ephraim Longworth and Donald McKinlay were full-back partners at Liverpool for eighteen years from 1910 to 1928.

Dave Clement played for QPR against Watford twice on the same day. On the morning of Saturday 21 May 1966 he played at centre half in a South-East Counties League game and in the afternoon was at right-back when QPR met the Hornets in a Football Combination match.

Every one of Wolves' forty-strong professional staff for the 1936/37 season was a bachelor.

Tommy Lawton and Len Shackleton both played two full games on Christmas Day, 1940. Lawton starred for Everton against Liverpool in the morning and guested for Tranmere Rovers against Crewe Alexandra in the afternoon, while Shackleton lined up for both Bradford clubs, City (as a guest) in the morning and Park Avenue in the afternoon.

When fifteen-year-old Stephen Briggs from Stainforth near Doncaster, at 4ft 9ins tall and 6st 7lbs in weight, became an apprentice professional with Huddersfield Town in February 1971, he ranked as the smallest and lightest player ever signed by a professional League club.

On 11 April 1892, four Scots – Donald Gow, Harry Gardiner, Willie Groves and Tom McInnes – played for the Football League against the Scottish League.

Trevor Ford, Ray Daniel, Ivor Allchurch, John Charles, Mel Charles and Barrie Jones all spent their early careers with Swansea Town, all moved to English clubs, all became full Welsh internationals and all were later signed by Cardiff City.

During the 1940s and 1950s West Bromwich Albion ran nine different teams and winger Reg Cutler played for them all.

Only four players are believed to have appeared in a competitive football match in England wearing glasses. They are Stanley Bourne of West Ham United, who played between 1906 and 1911; Scottish international Alex Raisbeck of Stoke,

Striker Jason Scotland was born in Trinidad, played for Dundee United and St Johnstone, scored his first League goal on an English ground (Boundary Park, Oldham) and now plays in Wales for Swansea City.

Liverpool, Partick Thistle and Hamilton Academical, who starred from the late 1890s up to 1912; England international goalkeeper James Frederick Mitchell of Blackpool, Preston North End and Manchester City, who played either side of the First World War; and the 2005 Dutch international midfielder Edgar Davids (Tottenham).

Accrington Stanley fielded an entire team of Scottish-born players in 1955/56.

In the 1920s Aston Villa had four full-backs whose Christian name was Tommy: Lyons, Smart, Mort and Weston. Goalkeeper Jackson, centre halves Ball and Jones and a centre forward, Waring, were also named Tom.

Former England centre half Ken Brown drew weekly wages from two Football League clubs at the same time. In season 1967/68 he was West Ham's pools organiser during the week and played for Torquay United on match days.

On 1 October 1896, full-back Bob Crompton signed for Blackburn Rovers, with whom he remained as a player until 30 May 1920. Crompton was also the first footballer to own his own car, in season 1907/08.

Released by Swansea Town in May 1928, full-back Roy John decided to try his luck as a goalkeeper with Walsall. He went on to win 13 caps for Wales and returned to Swansea during the First World War.

Jimmy Rimmer and Carlos Satori, players together at Manchester United between 1968 and 1971, were born on the same day, 10 February 1948.

Comedian George Robey was amateur with Millwall before the First World War; Wimbledon tennis champion Fred Perry was registered with Arsenal in 1934/35 and boxer Joe Louis signed amateur forms for Liverpool in 1944.

In 1956/57, Rhyl Athletic had three players named Denis Wilson on their books and two named Billy Hughes.

On the morning of Saturday 20 February 1922, Bill Poyntz got married. In the afternoon he scored a hat-trick for Leeds United against Leicester City. On Saturday 30 October 1954 Bill Holmes did the same thing, scoring a hat-trick for Southport against Carlisle United to celebrate tying the knot.

Premiership

The biggest win so far recorded in the Premiership is 9-0 by Manchester United over Ipswich Town at Old Trafford in March 1995. Manchester United also hold the record for the biggest away win – 8-1 at Nottingham Forest in February 1999.

Crystal Palace had a run of nine Premiership games without scoring during the 1994/95 season.

Leeds United did not win a single away game in 1992/93, and likewise Derby County in 2007–08.

Manchester United's Ruud van Nistelrooy set a Premiership record in 2003/04 by scoring in ten consecutive matches, netting a total of 15 goals in that run.

Swindon Town conceded a record 100 Premiership goals in 1993/94.

Manchester United hold the record for the most goals scored – 97 in 2002/03.

The fewest number of goals conceded in a Premiership season is 15 by Chelsea in 2004/05. Arsenal conceded 17 in 1997/98.

Derby County recorded only one win in 38 Premiership games in season 2007–08. Crystal Palace had recorded just two wins in 1997–98 and Sunderland four in 2002–03.

Most Premiership wins in a season is 29 by Chelsea in 2004–05 and 2005–06. Chelsea have also amassed the most points – 95 in 2004-05.

Arsenal hold the record for the fewest number of defeats – 0 in 2003/04.

The lowest points tally has so far has been 11, registered by Derby County in season 2007–08.

Ipswich Town in 1994–95 and Derby County in 2007–08 share the record for most defeats in a Premiership season – total 29.

Chelsea went a record 86 home games without defeat from March 2004 until November 2008 when Liverpool won 1–0 at Stamford Bridge.

Arsenal won 14 Premiership games in succession in seasons 2001/02 and 2002/03.

Manchester United won the Premiership title three seasons running from 1998 to 2001.

Alan Shearer scored a record 260 Premiership goals during his career which ended in 2006 (112 for Blackburn, 148 for Newcastle).

In 2004–05 Manchester United became the first club to gain 1,000 Premiership points and the following season they became the first to score 1,000 Premiership goals.

Andy Cole, for Newcastle United in 1993/94, and Alan Shearer, for Blackburn Rovers in 1994/95, share the record of scoring the most Premiership goals in one season, with 34. These same two players also share the record for scoring the most goals in one match – five – Cole for Manchester United against Ipswich Town in March 1995, Shearer for Newcastle United against Sheffield Wednesday in September 1999.

Arsenal scored in each of their thirty-eight Premiership games in 2002/03 – a record. They also claimed a record in 2001/02 when they won eight consecutive away games.

Seven clubs – Arsenal, Aston Villa, Chelsea, Everton, Liverpool, Manchester United and Tottenham – have competed in every Premiership season (1992-2005).

Chelsea won 10 successive away Premiership games in 2008–09.

West Bromwich Albion became the first club to escape relegation from the Premiership after being bottom of the table at Christmas. The Baggies achieved the 'Great Escape' in 2005 under manager Bryan Robson.

Arsenal holds the record for the longest unbeaten run – 49 matches.

Promotion & Relegation

Ups

Three teams, Birmingham City, Luton Town and Rotherham United, finished the 1954/55 Second Division season locked together at the top of the table with 54 points each. Birmingham and Luton were subsequently promoted, both having a better goal average than the Millers. This was the first time such a thing had occurred.

Chester, elected to the Third Division (North) in 1931, had to wait until 1975 before gaining their first promotion – the longest of any club in the competition.

When Port Vale won the Third Division (North) title in 1953/54, they did so by a record margin of 11 points. They suffered only 3 defeats in 46 games.

Arsenal have only officially gained promotion to the top flight once, in 1904, and actually played in the Second Division from 1913 to 1919. Since then they have always been in the top division of English football.

Wolves have won the First, Second, Third, Third (North) and Fourth Division titles.

Grimsby Town have won the championship (and ultimate promotion) of four divisions: Second, Third, Third (North) and Fourth.

Plymouth Argyle finished runners-up in Third Division (South) six seasons in a row in the 1920s. They finally gained a place in the Second Division in 1930 after winning the title.

By beating Preston North End 5-1 in their last game, Portsmouth pipped Manchester City, who defeated Bradford City 8-0, by just 0.005 of a goal to gain promotion as runners-up from the Second Division in 1926/27. City were promoted the following season.

When Northampton Town won promotion from the Fourth Division to the First in successive seasons between 1962/63 and 1964/65, four players – Mike Everitt, Terry Branston, Derek Leck and Barry Lines – appeared in all four divisions. Branston subsequently moved to Luton Town and helped the Hatters gain promotion from the Fourth Division to the Second before going on to help Lincoln City successfully apply for re-election.

Coventry City have won the championship of the Second, Third and Third (South) Divisions as well as finishing runners-up in the Third and Fourth Divisions.

In season 1972/73, the champions of all four divisions of the Football League came from Lancashire: Liverpool (First Division), Burnley (Second Division), Bolton Wanderers (Third Division) and Southport (Fourth Division).

The first club to win promotion after having successfully applied for re-election the previous year was Grimsby Town in 1955/56. York City followed suit nine seasons later.

In just nine years Wimbledon rose from the Southern League in 1976/77 to the top of the First Division in September 1986. Less than two years later they won the FA Cup.

Downs

Founder members of the Football League Aston Villa and Blackburn Rovers both suffered relegation for the first time in season 1935/36.

In 1976/77, Bobby Owen played for two relegated clubs, Carlisle United and Northampton Town, and also for Workington who finished bottom of the Fourth Division.

On the last day of the 1927/28 season no less than twelve clubs in the First Division faced the threat of relegation. In the end only seven points separated nineteen clubs with Derby County finishing fourth on 44 points while Middlesbrough were bottom on 37. Spurs were also relegated with 38 points.

Huddersfield Town won 14 of their 42 League games in 1955/56 and were relegated from the First Division with 35 points. In 1969/70, Crystal Palace won only six matches, gaining 27 points, yet still managed to stay up.

Reading were relegated to the Fourth Division for the first time in their centenary year of 1971.

Manchester City entertained Luton Town on the last day of the 1982/83 season. Whoever won would stay in the First Division. The Hatters, managed by David Pleat, grabbed the glory with a 1-0 scoreline, sending City down.

Fulham finished bottom of the First Division in 1967/68 and bottom of the Second Division the following season.

Manchester City were relegated from the First Division in 1937/38, despite scoring 80 goals. Five points covered the bottom thirteen clubs that season and City went down after losing their final match 1-0 at Huddersfield, who stayed up by virtue of that victory.

Between 1929 and 1935 goalkeeper Tom Poskett was with Grimsby Town, Lincoln City and Notts County in that order, and in turn all three were relegated.

West Bromwich Albion were relegated to the Second Division for the first time in their history at the end of their initial season at The Hawthorns, 1900/01.

Bristol City were relegated from the First Division to the Fourth in successive seasons: 1979/80-1981/82.

In the Second Division in 1978/79, Sheffield United scored more goals (52) than champions Crystal Palace (51) yet were relegated.

Ups and Downs

Inside forward Redfern Froggatt played in three Sheffield Wednesday teams that were relegated from the First Division in 1951, 1955 and 1958. He was a member of four of the Owls' promoted sides as well, in 1950, 1952, 1956 and 1959.

Tony Coleman also had mixed fortunes. Between 1966 and 1971 he helped Manchester City win both the Second and First Division titles, the FA Cup and the European Cup-Winners' Cup but played for Sheffield Wednesday and Blackpool when they were relegated from the top flight.

Inside forward Willie Carlin served seven different clubs over a twelve-year period and all of them were involved in either promotion or relegation issues. He started out with Liverpool but after their promotion from the Second Division in 1962 he joined Halifax Town, who were soon relegated to the Fourth. He then helped Carlisle United climb out of the Third in 1965 and was with Sheffield United when they went down from the First in 1968 before playing for both Derby County and then Leicester City when they rose from the Second Division in 1969 and 1971 respectively. His fifth and final promotion came with Notts County when they entered the Third Division in 1973.

In 1955/56 Yorkshire clubs Huddersfield Town and Sheffield United were relegated from the First Division and were replaced by Leeds United and Sheffield Wednesday. It is the only time in Football League history that the relegated pair and the two promoted teams have all come from the same county.

Over a period of almost twenty years between 1948/49 and 1967/68, Stirling Albion were promoted six times and relegated six times.

Peterborough United were demoted from the Third Division at the end of the 1967/68 season as punishment for offering illegal payments to players.

Carlisle United topped the First Division table in 1974. Thirty years later they lost their Football League status, being relegated to the Nationwide Conference with York City, who had themselves been FA Cup semi-finalists in 1955.

In the 1936/37 season Manchester City were First Division Champions while Manchester United were relegated. A year later City were relegated while United were promoted as Second Division Champions. In 2001/02 West Bromwich Albion pipped Black Country neighbours Wolves for a place in the Premiership. The following season Albion were relegated and Wolves promoted but a year later the two clubs swapped places again.

In 1921/22 Barnsley missed promotion to the First Division by 0.075 of a goal. Ten years later a fraction of a goal caused their descent from the Second Division and in 1938 the Tykes went down again because of an inferior goal average – 0.78125 compared to Nottingham Forest's 0.78333.

Northampton Town rose from the Fourth to the First Division and then slipped all the way down again in the space of eight years from 1961 to 1969. Swansea City reached the First Division in 1981 but were back in the Fourth five years later.

Aston Villa were saved from having to apply for re-election to the Football League at the end of the 1889/90 season when a decision was made to suspend the rules!

With 96 goals, Manchester City scored more than any other Second Division club in 1938/39 but failed to gain promotion.

Referees

Birmingham MP Dennis Howell was the selected referee for the League game between Bristol Rovers and Lincoln City in November 1956, but he was forced to withdraw owing to an extended sitting of Parliament.

Referee Major Mandirin officiated in a record eight FA Cup finals: 1880, 1884, 1885, 1886, 1887, 1888, 1889 and 1890.

Prior to the 1888 FA Cup final between the favourites Preston North End and underdogs West Bromwich Albion, Mandirin was asked by North End if they could be photographed with the trophy, so confident were they of winning. 'Hadn't you best win it first?' asked the referee. Albion upset the odds by winning 2-1.

John Douglas refereed four games in one day, the first in Dulwich (kick-off 6.45 a.m.), the second at Chiswick (kick-off 10.30 a.m.), the third at Pinner (kick-off 3.00 p.m.) and his last in Olympia (kick-off 8.00 p.m.).

Up until 1891, umpires were used rather than linesmen. These have now been replaced with assistant referees!

The first time a referee used a whistle was for the Sheffield v. Nottingham Forest friendly in 1878.

Referee Gordon Kew sent off seven players in League games in 1972/73 – a record at that time.

Policeman-referee Peter Willis was the first official to send a player off in an FA Cup final, dismissing Manchester United's Kevin Moran against Everton in 1985. Earlier, in season 1979/80, Willis had booked eight players in the Doncaster Rovers v. Hereford United League game at Belle Vue, seven from the visiting team.

After a goal had been controversially disallowed during a League match in Livramento, Brazil, in the early 1960s, an irate fan raced onto the pitch and knocked out the referee. Another supporter then came onto the field of play and stabbed the first fan, only for a third spectator to come forward to shoot the second with a revolver.

In 1962 a pretty student nurse from Prague, seventeen-year-old Syle Gregrova, became the first woman football referee in Europe.

Six Dartmoor prisoners coached by the Devon FA passed the football referees' written examination in 1962 with an average mark of 96%.

Referee Mr E.D. Smith (Sunderland) appeared on the radio prior to the 1947 FA Cup final and stated that the chance of the ball bursting again like it had in the previous year's final was a million to one. Yes, you've guessed it, it burst again. Charlton Athletic were playing on both occasions.

During a minor league game in Farnborough, Kent, the referee booked all twenty-two players and one of his linesmen.

Macclesfield referee Jack Parker officiated in the two Football League games between Chester and Tranmere Rovers in 1950/51. He was injured in both and left the field on each occasion.

Two Port Vale players – Tom Kirkham and Jim Mason – became top-line referees, officiating at cup finals and international matches.

The youngest referee ever to control an FA Cup final was thirty-two-year-old Mr H. Bamlett of Gateshead who was in charge of the 1914 clash between Burnley and Liverpool at Crystal Palace.

It was not until 1950 that the rule was introduced whereby an international match should be refereed by someone from a neutral country.

There were two referees on the field at the same time, each looking after one half of the pitch, at the England v. The Rest international trial match at The Hawthorns in March 1935. Two months later the same method of refereeing was again tried out when a Football League XI met West Bromwich Albion in a friendly at the same venue. At the League's AGM in 1937 it was proposed that two referees should be utilised in League games, but the proposal was defeated.

On 13 September 1999, football history was made when all three officials for the Conference game between Kidderminster Harriers and Nuneaton were women: Wendy Toms was the referee and Janie Frampton and Amy Raynor were assistant referees.

Results

League Action

Grimsby Town are the only team to have won home and away League matches with a scoreline of 6-5. They beat West Bromwich Albion at The Hawthorns in April 1937 and Burnley at Blundell Park in October 2002.

In season 1898/99, Millwall's reserve team produced one of the most incredible lists of results imaginable for a first-class club by winning all of their 30 League games and scoring 212 goals while conceding only 13.

All eleven First Division matches on 10 December 1955 ended in home wins, as did all twelve Third Division encounters played over the weekend of 18-19 October 1968.

Rangers won all their matches in the Scottish League in 1898/99, gaining the maximum 36 points.

In November 1935, a week after losing 5-0 at Rotherham, York City recorded a remarkable 7-5 home League win over Mansfield Town – their highest score of the season.

In 1977/78 Leicester City set club records for the most League defeats (25), the least number of goals scored (26), the fewest home wins (4), the lowest number of points (22) and the worst goal difference (-44). They were relegated from the First Division in last place.

Prior to gaining entry to the Football League Peterborough United did not lose a home game in the Midland League for four years from 1956 to 1960.

Celtic were undefeated between mid-November 1915 and late April 1917, during which time they played a total of 63 games.

Blackpool won only one home League game in 1966/67 – but it was quite a victory, as they thrashed Newcastle United 6-0 in late October.

When Everton won the League Championship in 1931/32 they had a run of seven consecutive home victories that produced 47 goals. The scorelines read 9-3, 8-1, 7-2, 9-2, 5-1, 5-0 and 4-2.

In January 1939, after losing 6-1 at New Brighton and 6-2 at Bradford City, Hull City won their next match 11-1 against Carlisle United – their biggest win in the Football League.

Millwall is the only Football League club to have been unbeaten at home in a full League season in four different divisions.

In 1933/34 Newcastle United won 7-3 at Everton on Boxing Day and beat Liverpool 9-2 at St James' Park on New Year's Day but still went down to the Second Division.

In 1935/36 Chester beat York City 12-0, Barrow 4-2 and New Brighton 8-2 in successive League games, clocking up 24 goals in 3 matches.

Bradford City beat both Tranmere Rovers and Barrow by eight goals to nil in the space of three days in March 1929.

In contrast, Wrexham beat Carlisle United 8-1 and then lost 7-3 at Stockport County in successive League games in March 1933.

In 1930 two League games had 7-5 scorelines in favour of the away team: Blackburn Rovers won at Sheffield United while Preston North End defeated Millwall at The Den.

Bristol City had to beat Nottingham Forest in the last League game of the 1909/10 season to avoid relegation. They did so by 4-0 with John Cowell scoring their goals.

In April 1895, West Bromwich Albion needed to beat Sheffield Wednesday by at least five goals to avoid relegation to the Second Division. Albion won 6-0 just to make certain!

Newport County lost 7-2 at home to West Bromwich Albion and 13-0 away at Newcastle in successive Second Division matches in September/October 1946.

Manchester United won their first ten League matches in 1985/86.

Ardwick, now Manchester City, beat Bootle 7-0 in their first ever League encounter, a Second Division match played in August 1892.

Newcastle United were 6-0 winners over Arsenal in their first ever home League game in September 1893.

Hibernian won 11-1 at Airdrie in a Scottish League game in 1959/60, while the biggest away win in the Football League First Division is 9-1, achieved by Wolves at Cardiff in 1955/56. Sheffield United beat Port Vale 10-0 in the Potteries in 1892/93 for the League's biggest away win while Sunderland also won 9-1 at rivals Newcastle United in 1908/09 (Second Division).

Bolton Wanderers went 26 League games without a win between 31 April and 10 January 1903. They drew 3 and lost 23.

In season 1935/36, there were 259 home wins, 92 away wins and 111 draws in both the First and Second Divisions of the Football League – the only time the records of these two divisions have been identical.

Reading beat Crystal Palace 10-2 and Southend United 7-2 in successive home League games in September 1946.

All eleven First Division matches played on 10 December 1955 ended in home wins.

Fulham lost eighteen League games by the odd goal in 1951/52 and were relegated to the Second Division.

In October 1925, Manchester City beat Burnley 8-3 at home and a week later lost by the same score at Sheffield United.

Over the Christmas period of 1963 West Ham United lost 8-2 at home to Blackburn Rovers yet forty-eight hours later won the return fixture 3-1 at Ewood Park.

Five teams have won all their home League games in one season. The teams to have accomplished the feat in the Second Division are Liverpool (fourteen games) in 1893/94; Bury (fifteen games) in 1894/95; Sheffield Wednesday (seventeen games) in 1899/1900 and Birmingham City (seventeen games) in 1902/03. Brentford won all twenty-one of their home Third Division (South) games in 1929/30.

Rotherham United won their first twenty home League matches after the Second World War.

Cambridge United went thirty-one matches without a League win in 1983/84.

Darwen in 1898/99 and Walsall in 1988/98 both suffered fifteen successive League defeats – a joint record.

Gillingham played out fifty-two League and cup games at home without defeat between April 1963 and April 1965.

In 1946/47, Doncaster Rovers won the Third Division (North) title with 72 points by winning 33 and drawing 6 of their 42 matches and scoring 123 goals. The following season they were relegated after amassing just 29 points from 9 wins and 11 draws, scoring only 40 goals.

In 1922/23 Second Division sides Southampton and Hull City had identical records: 14 wins, 14 draws and 14 defeats. Saints finished higher with a goal average of 40-40 against Hull's 43-45.

In 1938/39 Third Division (North) Rotherham United won 17 and lost 17 of their 42 League games. Their goal average was 64-64, they obtained 42 points and finished eleventh out of twenty-two in the table.

Cup Competitions

The biggest win ever recorded in a competitive game in Britain is 36-0 by Arbroath over Bon Accord in a Scottish Cup tie in 1885. John Petrie scored thirteen goals and Arbroath's 'keeper Ned Doig never touched the ball in the one-sided contest. On that same day, Dundee Harp beat Aberdeen Rovers 35-0, also in the Scottish Cup.

The biggest FA Cup win so far recorded in England was achieved by Preston North End, who beat luckless Hyde 26-0 in the 1887/88 competition.

Derby County won a record nine FA Cup games in 1946/47.

Liverpool completed a unique cup treble in 2001, winning the League Cup, FA Cup and UEFA Cup. They played a total of 23 matches of which 17 were won, 4 drawn and 2 lost. The Reds scored 55 goals and conceded 19. They also won the FA Charity Shield and the European Super Cup in that year.

In the second round of the League Cup in 1980/81 Watford lost the first leg 4-0 at Southampton but won the return leg at Vicarage Road by 7-0 for an aggregate 7-4 victory.

When Manchester United won the FA Cup in 1948 they defeated six First Division clubs to do it: Aston Villa, Liverpool, Charlton Athletic, Preston North End, Derby County and, in the final, Blackpool. They scored 22 goals in these matches.

The record away win in the FA Cup is 14-0, by Nottingham Forest at Clapton in season 1890/91.

League and Cup

Leicester City and Luton Town opposed each other four times in 1948/49 (two League games, two FA Cup matches). A total of twenty-two goals were scored – both Second Division encounters finished level at 1-1, while City won a fifth-round FA Cup replay 5-3 after a 5-5 draw.

Leicester City won ten consecutive League and cup matches in a sixteen-game unbeaten run in 1962/63.

Top Scores in British Senior Competitions

English Premiership
4 March 1995
Manchester United 9-0 Ipswich Town

First Division
4 April 1892
West Bromwich Albion 12-0 Darwen
21 April 1909
Nottingham Forest 12-0 Leicester Fosse

Second Division
5 October 1946
Newcastle United 13-0 Newport County

Third Division
5 September 1987
Gillingham 10-0 Chesterfield

Third Division (South)
13 April 1936
Luton Town 12-0 Bristol Rovers

Third Division (North)
3 February 1934
Stockport County 13-0 Halifax Town

Fourth Division
26 December 1962
Oldham Athletic 11-0 Southport

FA Cup
15 October 1887
Preston North End 26-0 Hyde

League Cup
23 September 1986
Liverpool 10-0 Fulham
25 October 1983
West Ham United 10-0 Bury

Scottish Premier League
26 March 1979
Aberdeen 8-0 Motherwell

Scottish First Division
26 October 1895
Celtic 11-0 Dundee

Scottish Second Division
24 October 1950
Airdrie 15-1 Dundee Wanderers

Scottish Cup
12 September 1885
Arbroath 36-0 Bon Accord

International
18 February 1882
England 13-0 Ireland

Scottish Facts

Jimmy McGrory scored a record 468 goals in 445 senior games for Celtic between 1921 and 1937. His total in League football was 395 in 378 outings – another record, surpassing Steve Bloomer's 352 League goals in 599 outings for Derby County and Middlesbrough before the First World War. McGrory netted 50 times for the Bhoys in 1935/36 and in January 1928 he fired home a record eight goals in a game, including a hat-trick in the opening nine minutes, when Celtic beat Dunfermline Athletic 8-0 in the League at Parkhead.

In comparison to McGrory, Ally McCoist scored 355 goals in 581 competitive appearances for Rangers between 1983 and 1999. His League haul was 251 in 418 games.

Scotland's first League hat-trick was scored by John 'Kitey' McPherson for Rangers against Cambuslang in August 1890. The 'Gers won 6-2.

Celtic won the European Cup and all three Scottish domestic trophies in 1966/67. In that same season arch-rivals Rangers lost in the final of the European Cup-Winners' Cup, lost to Celtic in the League Cup final, came second in the League Championship and were eliminated from the Scottish Cup by underdogs Berwick Rangers. The Bhoys also won the Glasgow Cup.

Glasgow Rangers failed to appear for the replay of the Scottish Cup final in 1879, so the trophy was awarded to Vale of Leven.

Henrik Larsson, despite suffering a double fracture to his leg in October 1999 that sidelined him for almost seven months, ended his Celtic career in May 2004 with a total of 169 goals in 232 League games.

The referee who booked St Johnstone defender Don McVicar during a 1987 League game with Meadowbank Thistle was none other than – Don McVicar!

In 2003/04 Celtic created a new Scottish record by gaining twenty-five consecutive League wins, beating the previous record set by Morton.

A total of 71 goals were scored on one day in just two Scottish Cup games in 1885. Arbroath beat Bon Accord 36-0 and Dundee Harp beat Aberdeen Rovers 35-0.

Celtic scored 323 League goals over a period of three seasons. Their tallies were 106 in 1965/66, 111 in 1966/67 and 106 in 1967/68. In all games during this period the Bhoys netted a total of 496 goals at competitive level.

After his fifth sending-off, thirty-five-year-old Rangers and Scotland player Willie Woodburn was suspended indefinitely by the SFA on 14 September 1954. He never played again.

Owing to the atrocious arctic weather conditions, Celtic played only one football match between 25 January and 15 March 1947.

Again, due to the freezing weather conditions, Rangers managed to complete just one League game (against Celtic) between 1 January and 9 March 1963. This season started on 11 August and finished on 27 May.

In 2003/04, East Stirlingshire conceded 118 goals in 38 Scottish Third Division matches and ended the season with a goal difference of -88.

In September 2001 Celtic – for the first time in the club's history – fielded a team without a single Scotsman in it when they entertained Dunfermline Athletic at Parkhead. They won 3-1.

Celtic used three different goalkeepers during their League game with Hibernian in February 1950. Hibs won 4-1.

Rangers used six different goalkeepers during the 1895/96 season.

Goalkeeper Willie Robb made 241 consecutive appearances for Rangers between April 1920 and October 1925.

Bill Hogg was the first England international signed by Rangers, arriving from Sunderland in May 1909.

The first non-European to play for Rangers was the Egyptian Mohammed Latif, appearing against Hibernian in September 1935.

The Dane Carl Hansen was the first foreigner to score in an Old Firm derby, doing so for Rangers in January 1923.

Stirling Albion failed to score in any of their last thirteen Scottish League games in season 1980/81.

The first Scottish League game to be played under floodlights saw Rangers beat Queen of the South 8-0 in March 1956. Don Kitchenbrand scored a hat-trick for the 'Gers.

Scotland's first Player of the Year was Celtic's Billy McNeill in 1964/65. John Greig of Rangers was the second, in 1965/66.

Marco Negri scored in ten consecutive Premier League games for Rangers in 1997/98 – a club record.

Charlie Tully scored direct from a corner for Celtic against Falkirk in a Scottish Cup tie in February 1953. He was ordered to retake the kick and scored for a second time. The Bhoys won 3-2.

Falkirk played out 17 League draws in each of seasons 1921/22 and 1922/23 when finishing fifth and fourth respectively in the Scottish First Division.

A British record crowd of 149,547 witnessed the international match between Scotland and England at Hampden Park in April 1937. The Scots won 3-1.

Celtic played 8 games in eleven days between 19 and 30 April 1909. They won 5, drew 2 and lost 1 and pipped Dundee by a point to take the League title.

Celtic won the Scottish Cup in 1910/11 without conceding a goal in the competition.

On 15 April 1916, Celtic played two League matches on the same day and won them both, beating Raith Rovers 6-0 in the afternoon and Motherwell 3-1 in the evening.

Celtic went 62 League games without defeat from November 1915 to April 1917.

Hearts defender Graeme Hogg was suspended for ten matches in 1994 after being sent off in a pre-season friendly against Raith Rovers for punching his own teammate Craig Levene.

Kenny Dalglish was the first player to score 100 League goals in both Scotland and England. He scored 112 for Celtic and 118 for Liverpool.

Stirling Albion beat Selkirk 20-0 in a Scottish Cup tie in December 1984.

In 1966/67 Joe McBride scored 35 goals in only 26 games for Celtic. He missed half the season through injury.

Celtic became the first club in Scotland to amass over 100 points in the top flight. They gained 103 in 2001/02.

Raith Rovers scored a record 142 goals in 34 League games in the 1937/38 season. Hearts claimed 132 in 1957/58.

Luckless Brechin City lost 10-0 three times in the space of seven weeks in 1937/38. They conceded 139 goals during the campaign.

In September 1975, Celtic players missed four penalties in four games.

Five players, one from Celtic, four from Rangers, were sent off in two Old Firm derbies in the space of a week in March 1991.

In 1947/48, Henry Morris scored 62 League and cup goals for East Fife.

Right-winger Jack Buchanan found the net in eleven successive First Division games for Clyde in 1952/53.

West Bromwich Albion did not have a single Scotsman on their books between 1907 and 1937. Tommy Dilly was transferred to Everton in 1907 and after that Baggies' chairman Billy Bassett refused to sign another Scottish-born player. He died in 1937 and almost immediately Albion signed Glaswegian George Dudley.

Two Englishmen, Bert Lee from Dorset and Bill Lyon from Cheshire, skippered their respective teams to victory in the Scottish Cup final – Lee with Dundee in 1910 and Lyon with Celtic in 1937.

Hearts scored 31 Scottish Cup goals in 1938/39, yet still failed to reach the quarter-final stage.

Scotsmen scored 72 of Preston North End's 76 League and FA Cup goals in 1937/38.

Paul Sturrock scored a then-record five goals in a Scottish Premier match for Dundee United against Morton in November 1984.

Celtic beat Rangers 7-1 in the Scottish League Cup final of October 1957 – the greatest ever margin of victory in a major domestic final in the United Kingdom.

Twenty goals were scored in the two League games featuring Dundee's two clubs on 21 February 1959. Dundee lost 6-4 at home to St Mirren in the First Division while United crashed 8-2 away to Berwick Rangers in the Second Division.

Hamilton Academical, formed in 1874, are the only senior club in Great Britain to be named after a school – Hamilton Academy.

In 1990/91 it was possible for Glasgow Rangers to field a full team without including a single Scotsman. There were nine English players, including internationals Chris Woods, Gary Stevens, Trevor Steven, Terry Butcher, Mark Hateley and Mark Walters, as well as Russian Oleg Kuznetsov and Dutchman Pieter Huistra.

Before Aberdeen were nicknamed the 'Dons' they were called the 'Whites' and then the 'Wasps'.

Fifteen out of nineteen professionals registered with Accrington Stanley in 1955/56 were Scotsmen and on several occasions during the season the team was made up entirely of Scots.

East Fife are the only Second Division side ever to win the Scottish Cup, beating Kilmarnock 4-2 in the 1938 final.

Scotsmen Hughie Ferguson and Jim Henderson both scored five goals in League games for Cardiff City.

The first Scotsman to score at Wembley was John Reid Smith, for Bolton Wanderers against West Ham United in the 1923 FA Cup final. Smith was also the first Scot to win English and Scottish domestic cup finals, achieving the latter with Kilmarnock in 1920.

3 goals were scored in the last 100 seconds of the Division Two game between Brechin City and Arbroath in February 2005. Arbroath led 3-2 but goals by Hamilton and Callaghan earned the home side a 4-3 victory.

Service

Joe Reader was associated with West Bromwich Albion for sixty-six years from 1885 to 1950. Initially a goalkeeper, and capped by England in that position, he retired in 1901 to become trainer-coach at The Hawthorns, and later worked on the ground staff until he was eighty-four years of age.

Fred Bradley was an official with Stoke City for forty-three years from 1924 to 1967 and during that time he never watched a match. He was the club's official commissionaire whose sole duties were at the front entrance to the Victoria Ground, preventing him from seeing any of the action out on the field.

Substitutes

On Boxing Day 2003, seventeen-year-old Will Hoskins came on as a sixty-first minute substitute for Rotherham United against Wigan Athletic and scored twice in three minutes to earn his side a 2-1 win.

West Bromwich Albion full-back Dennis Clarke was the first substitute to be used in an FA Cup final, replacing the injured John Kaye after ninety minutes of the 1968 showdown with Everton, which the Baggies won 1-0.

Trainers

Between the First and Second World wars Scotsman Billy Barr trained twelve League clubs: Huddersfield Town, Kilmarnock, Third Lanark, Port Vale, Raith Rovers, Sheffield Wednesday, Luton Town, Walsall, Coventry City, Bristol Rovers, Swindon Town and Exeter City.

George Walker was Sheffield United's trainer for thirty-six years from 1894 to June 1930 – a record unequalled anywhere in the world.

Jack Lewis trained three different FA Cup final teams in eleven years – Wolves (1893), Everton (1897) and Bolton Wanderers (1904).

Because of injuries Plymouth Argyle had to play their trainer, Bill Harper, in goal in League games against Sheffield Wednesday, Tottenham Hotspur and Blackburn Rovers in April 1939.

The Bournemouth trainer Harry Kinghorn was forty-eight years of age when he was asked to play at outside left in order to make up the team against Brentford in March 1929.

Transfers

English

Britain's first £1 million footballer was Trevor Francis, bought by Nottingham Forest boss Brian Clough from Birmingham City in February 1979. This came only a month after David Mills had become the first £500,000 player, Mills costing £516,000 when he left Middlesbrough for West Bromwich Albion. In February 1978 Manchester United had signed Gordon McQueen from Leeds for £498,000.

Britain's (and indeed the world's) first £1,000 transfer took place in 1905 when Alf Common left Sunderland for Middlesbrough. One journalist described the transfer as 'professionalism gone mad'.

Denis Law was the first British player to be transferred for a six-figure fee when he joined Manchester United from the Italian club Torino for £116,000 in August 1962.

Tony Hateley was the first player to transfer from one English club to another for £100,000 when he switched from Aston Villa to Chelsea in 1966.

In 1928 David Jack became the first £10,000 footballer when he joined Arsenal from Bolton Wanderers.

On 22 December 1971, Alan Ball was transferred from Everton to Arsenal in a deal he knew nothing about. He was told it was a Christmas present!

Blond striker Alun Evans became football's costliest teenager when he joined Liverpool from Wolves for £100,000 in September 1968.

Notts County twice broke the British transfer record, signing Tommy Lawton from Chelsea in November 1947 for £20,000 and transferring Jackie Sewell to Sheffield Wednesday for £34,000 in March 1951.

When Andy Cole was transferred from Bristol City to Newcastle United in March 1993 for £1.75 million he became the first graduate of the FA National School of Excellence to command a seven-figure fee.

Sunderland broke the club transfer record three times in three months between August and October 1979.

In 1933, Jim McCambridge played for three clubs in three different countries in three weeks: Bristol Rovers in England, Cardiff City in Wales and Ballymena in Northern Ireland.

1940s winger Jack Hays who played for Bradford City, Burnley and Bury, later transferred to the other Bury – Bury St Edmunds – as player-manager.

Gerry Daly was the first Republic of Ireland player to be transferred between two Football League clubs for a six-figure fee, moving from Manchester United to Derby County for £175,000 in 1977.

Scottish-born forward Frank Sharp was registered with three different clubs in two days in February 1969, moving from Carlisle United to Southport on loan on the eighteenth of the month and then transferring to Cardiff City twenty-four hours later.

Centre forward Johnny Ball played in three divisions of the Football League in six weeks: during September and October 1934 he turned out for Manchester United in the First Division, Huddersfield Town in the Second Division and Luton Town in the Third Division (North). This is a Football League record.

Centre forward Tommy Taylor was transferred from Barnsley to Manchester United in 1953 for £29,999 – because he didn't want to become a £30,000 player! United manager Matt Busby gave the odd pound to the tea lady at Old Trafford.

Bert Barlow was transferred from Wolves to Portsmouth in March 1939. A month later he scored for Pompey when they beat his former club 4-1 in the FA Cup final.

Another Wolves player, Stan Burton, was transferred to West Ham United for a record fee of £6,000 after playing in that 1939 FA Cup final. He then turned out for the Hammers in a League game against Manchester City before the end of the season.

Kevin Bremner played for five different clubs covering four divisions in 1982/83: Colchester United, Birmingham City, Wrexham, Plymouth Argyle and Millwall.

On 28 January 1948, Watford signed five Leicester City players: goalkeeper Calvert, half-backs Egglesden and Osborne and forwards Hartley and Cheney.

John Ball was transferred from First Division Manchester United to Second Division Huddersfield Town, and then to Luton Town in the Third Division (South) in the space of seven weeks in 1934.

Harry Jackson was transferred from Manchester City to Preston North End on Christmas Eve 1947 and exactly a year later he moved from Deepdale to another Lancashire club, Blackburn Rovers.

Scottish

Third Lanark transferred ten players to English clubs in 1963, including Alex Harley and Matt Gray to Manchester City and Dave Hilley to Newcastle United.

Alex Merrie was transferred from Scottish clubs to English clubs and back seven times in ten years from 1925 to 1935. He switched from St Mirren to Portsmouth to Ayr United to Hull City to Clyde to Crewe Alexandra to Brechin City to Aldershot. Afterwards he played for Cork in the Irish Republic and non-League Gloucester City.

Colin Stein was the first player to be involved in a £100,000 transfer between Scottish clubs, moving from Hibernian to Rangers in 1968.

Cameron Evans was transferred from Rangers to Sheffield United in November 1968 but within forty-eight hours he had returned to Ibrox Park 'homesick' after playing in just one second-team match for the Blades.

Overseas

The first player to be transferred for £1 million was Johan Cryuff, moving from Ajax to Barcelona in 1973.

In the summer of 1949, a player from Hungary was transferred to an Italian club for a doughnut-making machine!

The Wanderers

Goalkeeper John Burridge was associated with twenty-eight different clubs during a career that spanned over thirty years from 1968 to 1999. He was registered with Workington, Blackpool, Aston Villa, Southend United, Crystal Palace, Queens Park Rangers, Wolves, Derby County, Sheffield United, Southampton, Newcastle United (two spells), Hibernian, Scarborough (two spells), Lincoln City, Enfield, Aberdeen, Barrow, Dumbarton, Falkirk, Manchester City, Notts County, Witton Albion, Darlington, Grimsby Town, Gateshead, Northampton Town, Queen of the South and Blyth Spartans.

Joe Hooley was transferred seven times before his twenty-first birthday on Boxing Day 1959. He went on to assist seven other clubs before taking up coaching, first in Sudan and later in England, Iceland, Norway and Germany.

Centre forward Harry Crockford was transferred three times and played for four different League clubs in less than eight months in 1925, moving from Chesterfield to Gillingham to Accrington Stanley and to Walsall.

Inside forward Les Roberts served with seventeen different clubs between 1921 and 1938, although he did not appear in League games for all of them. He played for, in turn, Aston Villa, Chesterfield, Sheffield Wednesday, Bristol Rovers, Merthyr Town, Bournemouth, Bolton Wanderers, Swindon Town, Brentford, Manchester

City, Exeter City, Crystal Palace, Chester, Rochdale, Rotherham United, non-League Scunthorpe & Lindsey United and New Brighton. He amassed over 300 senior appearances as a utility forward.

Glider pilot-cum-ice cream manufacturer Abe Rosenthal was transferred from Tranmere Rovers to Bradford City in April 1947, to Oldham Athletic in March 1949, back to Tranmere in August 1949, on to Bradford City again in July 1952, to Tranmere once more in July 1954 and to Bradford City for a third time in July 1955.

Unusual Deals

In May 1950, Blackpool signed Billy Wright from a local junior club for a set of tangerine jerseys.

It was said that a freezer full of ice cream secured the transfer of Hugh McLenahan from Stockport County to Manchester United in 1927.

Centre half Alf Ridyard was transferred from West Bromwich Albion to QPR in 1938 while sitting in a barn on a nearby farm, having just milked a cow.

Jack Howe's transfer from Hartlepool United to Derby County was completed on platform three of Lincoln railway station in 1936.

In the 1930s Scottish intermediate club Mossend Celtic transferred Jack Spelton to Holytown United for thirty sheets of corrugated iron, so that they could erect a fence around their ground.

In 1935, Chesterfield manager Bill Harvey signed his namesake Bill Harvey from Eden Colliery FC.

Future Irish international striker Tony Casacarino joined Gillingham from Crockenill FC in 1981/82 in exchange for a set of tracksuits.

In November 1964, Scunthorpe United's Ian Lawther officially joined Brentford for £15,000 in the House of Commons. The appropriate forms were signed by the Bees' chairman Jack Dunnett who at the time was on duty as the MP for his Nottingham constituency.

Transfer Talk

Printed in the programme to play at right-back for Manchester City against Spurs at Maine Road on 5 November 1938 was Bert Sproston. However, Bert was suddenly transferred to the London club and actually played against his former colleagues in that game.

Stanley Matthews was forty-six when he returned to Stoke City from Blackpool in 1961. He went on to play League football until he was fifty.

On transfer deadline day in March 1967, Bill Atkins moved from Halifax Town to Stockport County with just four seconds remaining.

Billy Meredith was three months short of his forty-seventh birthday when he was transferred from Manchester United to Manchester City in 1921.

Charlie Buchan joined Arsenal from Sunderland for £2,000 in 1925 with the Gunners agreeing to pay an extra £100 to the Wearsiders for every goal he scored in his first season at Highbury. Buchan did well and cost the London club a further £2,000!

Goalkeeper Jimmy Prince had the unique experience of being transferred twice from the same non-League club to a major club with nearly ten years intervening. He left Northwich Victoria for Oldham Athletic in November 1927 but later returned to the Vics and was sold to Crewe Alexandra in July 1937.

In February 1925 centre forward Albert Pape was all set to play for Clapton Orient against Manchester United in a Second Division game at Old Trafford, but half an hour before the scheduled kick-off he was transferred to the opposition and went out and scored as United beat his former club 4-2.

In August 1956 Southern League side Cambridge United pulled off a major coup by signing the former Middlesbrough and England inside forward Wilf Mannion – who was then under a life ban imposed by the Football League!

In June 1929 Crystal Palace signed five Kettering Town players – a record at that time. The men were James Imrie, George Barrie, Peter Simpson, Andrew Dunsire and George Charlesworth.

In 1908 a £350 limit was placed on all transfer fees, but later in the year the ruling was withdrawn.

When Chelsea paid £15 million for Nicolas Anelka from Bolton Wanderers in January 2008, they had captured the most expensive player in the world at that time. His eight moves to various clubs since starting out with Paris St Germain, had aggregated transfer fees amounting to £87.2 million.

The World's Top 20 Transfers

1	Zinedine Zindane	Juventus to Real Madrid	2001	£46.5m
2	Luis Figo	Barcelona to Real Madrid	2000	£37.4m
3	Hernan Crespo	Parma to Lazio	2000	£35.7m
4	Gianluigi Buffon	Parma to Juventus	2001	£34m
5	Christian Vieri	Lazio to Inter Milan	1999	£31m
6	Rio Ferdinand	Leeds United to Manchester United	2002	£30m
7	Gaizka Mendieta	Valencia to Lazio	2001	£29m
8	Ronaldo	Inter Milan to Real Madrid	2002	£28.9m
9	Juan Sebastian Veron	Lazio to Manchester United	2001	£28.1m
10	Rui Costa	Fiorentina to AC Milan	2001	£28m
11	Wayne Rooney	Everton to Manchester United	2004	£25m*
12	David Beckham	Manchester United to Real Madrid	2003	£25m
13	Michael Essien	Lyon to Chelsea	2005	£25m
14	Didier Drogba	Marseilles to Chelsea	2004	£24m
15	Shaun Wright-Phillips	Manchester City to Chelsea	2005	£21m
16	Ruud van Nistelrooy	PSV Eindhoven to Manchester Utd	2001	£19m
17	Rio Ferdinand	West Ham United to Leeds United	2000	£18m
18	Jose Antonio Reyes	FC Sevilla to Arsenal	2004	£17.6m
19	Damien Duff	Blackburn Rovers to Chelsea	2003	£17m
20	Hernan Crespo	Inter Milan to Chelsea	2003	£16.8m

* Rising to £27m (Source: National Press) (as at September 2005)

Trophies

All five Wolves teams won a trophy in season 1957/58 – a British record. The seniors won the Football League title, the reserves triumphed in the Central League, the Third XI won the Birmingham League (First Division), the fourth team were victors of the Worcestershire Combination and the fifth team won the coveted FA Youth Cup.

Wartime Football

Syd Puddefoot scored 40 goals out of West Ham United's London Combination tally of 102 in season 1917/18.

Tommy Lawton scored a total of 336 goals while serving with four different clubs during the Second World War. Ephraim Dodds netted 289, including 228 for Blackpool, and Albert Stubbins weighed in with 234, 232 of which were for Newcastle United.

Dodds scored 65 out of his side's total of 183 in 1941/42 and 47 the following season. Stoke City's Tommy Sale scored 55 in 1941/42 and Joe Payne netted 50 for Chelsea in 1943/44. Harry 'Popeye' Jones scored 44 goals for West Bromwich Albion in 1939/40.

Irish international Peter Doherty scored for ten different clubs during the Second World War.

Blackpool scored a total of 910 goals in 298 wartime matches; Liverpool netted 831 in 300 games and Arsenal 806 in 287.

Blackpool, in fact, scored 183 in 1941/42 while Liverpool notched 149 goals in 1943/44 having claimed 138 the previous season.

Luton Town conceded 838 goals in wartime matches while Aberaman conceded 141 in season 1944/45, Southport 137 in 1944/45 and Stockport County 131 in 1942/43.

In 1945/46 five teams scored 100 or more goals in their respective Football League North and South Divisions: Aston Villa, Derby County, Newcastle United, Sheffield United and West Bromwich Albion.

Eight clubs conceded over 100 goals in 1945/46: Blackburn Rovers, Leeds United, Leicester City, Millwall, Newport County (who let in the most, 125), Plymouth Argyle, Southampton and Swansea Town.

Everton's Norman Greenhalgh appeared in 251 games for the Merseysiders in the Second World War. Ray Middleton made 250 in goal for Chesterfield.

Paddy O'Connor scored eleven goals for Belfast Celtic against Glenavon in January 1941.

Cricketer-footballer Leslie Compton scored six goals when Arsenal beat Clapton Orient 15-2 in February 1941.

Several players scored eight goals in wartime games, including Ephraim Dodds for Blackpool against Stockport in 1941, Jack Rowley for Wolves against Derby County in 1942, Leslie Compton for Civil Defence against FF Forces in 1941 and Tommy Crawley for Coventry City against Luton Town in 1940.

West Bromwich Albion players scored eight goals in thirty-two minutes against Luton Town in November 1941.

Bill Hullett scored seven goals for Lincoln City away to Mansfield Town in April 1942.

Ephraim Dodds scored in seventeen consecutive games for Blackpool from late August to mid-December 1941.

Stoke City's Stanley Matthews won 29 wartime caps for England during the Second World War. Everton's Joe Mercer gained 27 and Tommy Lawton 23. Lawton also scored 24 international goals while Ephraim Dodds top-scored for Scotland with 8.

Tommy Walker of Hearts gained the most Scottish caps during the Second World War, a total of 11. Wales' most-capped wartime players were the Birmingham duo of Don Dearson with 15 and Billy Hughes 14.

On three occasions during the Second World War clubs fielded complete teams of guest players – Northampton Town against Norwich City on 18 April 1942 and against Stoke City on 23 May 1942, and Aldershot against West Ham United on 23 January 1943. A total of seventeen guest players actually figured in that Northampton v. Norwich game in 1942.

The Army side that played against Swindon Town in March 1940 comprised eleven Bolton Wanderers players.

Notts County had sixty guests in 1943/44 and used a total of 129 players in season 1943/44 – both wartime records.

West Bromwich Albion lost 4-0 at Notts County in the first leg of a Wartime League Cup game in February 1941 but won the return leg 5-0 for an aggregate 5-4 victory.

Horace Crossthwaite of Stockport County missed only two out of 144 Regional games played by his club during WW1.

Top Wartime Scores

February 1919

Bristol Rovers 20-0 Great Western Railway

April 1916

Bristol City 20-1 ASC (White City)

December 1940

Norwich City 18-0 Brighton & Hove Albion

November 1940

Cardiff City 18-1 Army XI

April 1941

Civil Defence 17-2 FF Forces

November 1917

Stoke 16-0 Blackburn Rovers

February 1942

Portsmouth 16-1 Clapton Orient

April 1944

Bath City 16-1 Aberaman

March 1943

Netherlands 1-15 RAF

February 1941

Arsenal 15-2 Clapton Orient

February 1942

Blackpool 15-3 Tranmere Rovers

September 1919

Bristol Rovers 14-1 Discharged Soldiers

April 1918

Bristol City 14-2 RAF (Filton)

September 1918

Bristol City 13-0 Discharged Soldiers

November 1917

Bristol City 13-0 RFC (Filton)

March 1942

Army XI 0-13 Norwich City

August 1941

Manchester United 13-1 New Brighton

weight

During the period 1899-1902 Sheffield United's defence was recognised as being the heaviest in the land, with three of the players combined weighing roughly 53 stone – giant goalkeeper Bill 'Fatty' Foulke (22 stone) and full-backs Harry Thickett (17st) and Peter Boyle (14st). This trio appeared together in two FA Cup finals. Before he retired Foulke actually topped the 25-stone mark.

World Cup

Gerd Muller, with 14 goals in 1970 and 1974 holds the record as the leading scorer in World Cup finals tournaments. France's Just Fontaine netted 13 times and Brazilians Pelé and Ronaldo 12 apiece.

Hakan Sukar of Turkey has scored the fastest goal in World Cup finals, netting after just 10.8 seconds *v.* South Korea in 2002.

Vaclev Masek of Czechoslovakia scored after sixteen seconds against Mexico in the World Cup finals of 1962.

The average attendance at the 1994 World Cup final matches in USA was a record 66,604. When England won in 1966 the average turnout per game was 50,458.

Thomas Ravelli set a new Swedish record by winning his 110th full international cap for his country in the semi-finals of the 1994 tournament, against Brazil.

Italy's Mauro Tassotti was banned from eight internationals after being held responsible for breaking Luis Enrique's nose with his elbow in the quarter-final clash with Spain in 1994.

Ray Wilkins was the first England player sent off in the World Cup, dismissed against Morocco in June 1986.

Paul McGrath became Aston Villa's most capped player when he lined up for the Republic of Ireland against Holland in the 1994 World Cup finals in America.

Hector Castro, who scored for Uruguay in their 4-2 World Cup final victory over Argentina in 1930, played football with only one arm.

Brazilian winger Jairzinho was the first player to score in every round of the World Cup finals, doing so in Mexico in 1970.

The names of all thirteen the players who starred for Madagascar against Tunisia in a World Cup qualifier in May 2001 began with the letters 'Ra': Raharison (in goal); defenders Radafison (sub: Ralahajanahary), Rakotonbrabe, Radonamaha and Ratsimihalona; midfielders Randriamarozaka, Randrianaivo, Randrianoelison, Razafindrakoto and Rasoanaivo; and striker Railison (sub: Randriananteneina).

Other Soccer Oddities

From Here and There

The playing area of Port Vale's pitch in the 1950s was the largest in the Football League, measuring 120 yards by 80 yards.

Cyril Webster was a professional with Everton for ten years, from 4 May 1929 until 2 May 1939, and never played in a Football League game.

Seven League clubs changed their home ground between the two World Wars: Clapton Orient, Gateshead, Manchester City, Norwich City, Queens Park Rangers, Southend United and Watford.

In 1968, Tottenham Hotspur defender Roger Hoy searched high and low for the car of his choice – he finally got it, registration number HOY 762D.

On 25 November 1967, Chelsea banked over £2,500 from the sale of 62,586 programmes for their home League match against Manchester United (attendance 54,712). This was a new record which beat the previous best of 59,900 sales for the Chelsea–Manchester United League fixture on 12 March 1966. Chelsea were also the first club to report seasonal programme sales of over a million – 1,072,707 copies were sold in 1970/71, realising a total of £55,305.90.

Inside right Bobby Smith played in 28 Second Division matches for Doncaster Rovers in 1935/36 and failed to score a single goal out of his side's total of 51.

1960s Penarol star Alberto Spencer carried a real Pan-American tag: he was born in Ecuador of an English father, married a Chilean girl while living in Argentina and later played international football for Uruguay.

Not the same man, Wolves had a goalkeeper named Charlie Chaplin. Birmingham and Darlington possessed a full-back called Baden Powell; Peterborough United, Sheffield United and Wolves have had George Bernard Shaw; Anthony Eden served with Aston Villa; Neville Chamberlain assisted Port Vale and Stoke City; George Livingstone played for Manchester City, Manchester United, Celtic and Rangers; Bob Hope was with West Bromwich Albion, Birmingham City and Sheffield Wednesday; Winston Churchill assisted Chelsea; Julius Caesar was chairman of Watford; and George Washington Elliott was leading scorer for Middlesbrough in seven out of nine peacetime seasons between 1909 and 1924.

Mike England skippered Wales, Sam English played for Ireland, Don Welsh was capped by England, Eric Welsh represented Ireland, Harry Wales played for Scotland, Laurie Scott was right-back for England and Elisha Scott kept goal for Ireland, while Alan Brazil scored for Scotland.

The top five clubs in the First Division at the end of the 1914/15 season all came from Lancashire – Everton, Oldham Athletic, Blackburn Rovers, Burnley and Manchester City in that order.

George Flowers, Doncaster Rovers' twelfth man in an away Second Division match at Bradford City in March 1936, earned more money that afternoon than any of his colleagues who played in the match. He was called upon to act as a replacement linesman because the appointed one failed to turn up. Flowers received the regulation fee of £1 11s 6d while the players were paid 30s.

Ted Liddell is the only man in history who has held posts with seven different Football League clubs in the same city (London). He was a 1920s half-back with Clapton Orient and Arsenal, manager of Fulham from 1929 to 1931 and assistant

manager at West Ham United before working as a scout for Brentford, Chelsea and Tottenham, Hotspur.

Torquay United substitute Brian Hill came on for his namesake Brian Hill at half-time during the FA Cup tie against Nuneaton Borough in 1971.

In 1903, Arsenal were so hard up they arranged an archery tournament at their ground to raise money to pay the players.

In seasons 1959/60, 1960/61 and 1962/63 Birmingham City avoided relegation from the First Division by just two points in each case. In 1963/64 they escaped by one point and in 1961/62 by four points. In four of the five seasons they had to win their final League game to stay up.

Burton is the only English town or city that used to have two Football League clubs at the same time and now has none.

Wimbledon have won both the FA Amateur Cup and the FA Cup and Middlesbrough have won the Amateur Cup and the League Cup.

At Warwick races on Monday 30 March 1925, a horse called King Throstle won the first race, while the second was won by Top of the League. That very same afternoon, West Bromwich Albion – the Throstles – beat Sheffield United 2-1 and in doing so went to the top of the First Division table – a most remarkable coincidence!

There are only seven clubs who play football in Liechtenstein.

In 1899 a law was introduced stating that 'bad language' would be ruled as 'violent conduct' on the field of play. One of the first players to be sent off under this new rule was the famous West Bromwich Albion and England winger Billy Bassett.

In 1990, James Major, the son of John Major, soon to become Prime Minister, had an unsuccessful trial with Aston Villa.

Pre-First World War Bolton Wanderers full-back Jack Slater became Conservative MP for Eastbourne while Roy Hartle, Bolton Wanderers' 1950s full-back, was a Conservative councillor for the local Halliwell ward.

The brother of ex-Portsmouth, Blackburn Rovers, Aston Villa, Leicester City, Peterborough United Wolves and Ireland striker Derek Dougan was married on the same day as the Queen and Prince Phillip. Another brother was born on the same day as Prince Charles while the 'Doog' himself became the father of a boy twenty-four hours after the Queen had her fourth child.

Southend United spent a total of forty-six years in the Third Division, from 1920 when it was formed, until 1966.

Austin Morris was a registered player with Mansfield Town in the 1930s.

A football team can be altered 39,916,800 ways using the same eleven players – simply multiply 1 x 2 x 3 x 4 x 5 x 6 x 7 x 8 x 9 x 10 x 11. Playing an average of 40 matches a season it would take a million years to do it!

Owing to the arctic weather conditions that gripped the UK the 1946/47 football season started on 31 August and finished on 31 May.

The one-millionth Football League game took place on 15 March 1971 between Hartlepool United and Brentford at Victoria Park.

Liverpool competed for seven trophies in 1984/85 and didn't win one.

In 1980/81 Nottingham Forest went in search of six trophies and won just one – the FA Charity Shield.

In 1928/29 Yorkshire celebrated with three championship-winning teams: Sheffield Wednesday in the First Division, Middlesbrough in the Second Division and Bradford City in the Third Division (North), while Arsenal in the First, Brentford in the Second and Charlton Athletic in the Third (South) did the honours for London in 1934/35.

In 1895/96 Everton officials uncovered serious turnstile fraud and the club also witnessed one of the first outbreaks of football violence.

In 1953/54 four Midland clubs won prizes: Wolves won the League Championship, Leicester City the Second Division title, Port Vale the Third Division (North) and West Bromwich Albion the FA Cup.

After top dogs FC Croatia Zagreb had lost their national Cup tie 3-2 to the minnows of Dugo Selo, a Fourth Division side, the coach and his players were each fined £2,600 by the furious directors. Meanwhile, the players from the winning team collected a bonus of £38 each.

Mick Lambert is the only player to appear as a substitute in both a Lord's Test match and an FA Cup final, doing so for England against Australia in June 1968 (as a member of the Middlesex ground staff) and for Ipswich Town against Arsenal in 1978.

Former Welsh international centre forward Trevor Ford was on the field as a substitute for Glamorgan in the County cricket match against Nottinghamshire when Gary Sobers set a world record by hitting Malcolm Nash for six sixes in one over at Swansea in August 1968.

Having failed to play a single home game between 14 December 1962 and 2 March 1963, Halifax decided to open their Shay Ground to the public as an ice-skating rink.

On 25 April 1981, Stockport County arrived at Gigg Lane to take on Bury with only eight regular players. They played the first half with nine men, two more arrived for the second period and amazingly County went on to win 1-0.

Jack Darston took five wickets for Surrey against Middlesex at Lord's and kept goal for Brentford against Millwall on the same day – 30 August 1920.

Norwich City's Carrow Road ground took only eighty-two days to build. The work was completed in the summer of 1935.

The only Premiership player so far to have played first-class cricket is Steve Palmer – for Watford (in 1999/2000) and Cambridge University.

On 1 October 1938, in the wake of the Munich Agreement, Charlton Athletic's guests at their 4-4 home draw with Bolton Wanderers included the Prime Minister Neville Chamberlain and the Rector of Charlton.

Notts County's Andy Legg entered the Guinness Book of Records in August 1994 by recording the longest ever throw-in in first-class football by hurling the ball 41m.

The South African League game between Jomo Cosmos and Moroka Swallows in 1998 came to an abrupt end when several players were hit by a bolt of lightning.

Tragedy struck in the Republic of Congo, also in 1998, when the eleven players from one village team were all killed and around thirty spectators injured when lightning arrived mid-game.

Because of a colour clash, Blackburn Rovers players wore white evening dress shirts for their 1890 FA Cup final encounter with The Wednesday.

Manchester City were the first English club to win a domestic trophy and European prize in the same season, lifting the League Cup and European Cup-Winners' Cup in 1969/70.

There was not one shot on goal during the Stoke City v. Burnley League game of April 1898. It goes without saying that the final score was 0-0.

West Bromwich Albion did not have a single shot or header on goal in their Premiership game at Manchester City in December 2004, yet still managed a 1-1 draw courtesy of an own goal by City defender Richard Dunne.

Bradford City were elected to the Football League in 1903 before they had got a team together. Chelsea followed suit in 1905.

In the period between the two world wars Rotherham United were the only team that failed to turn up for a League game. Fog prevented them from reaching Hartlepool United's ground on 22 December 1934.

In 1957 Everton became the first club to install under-soil heating.

Russian billionaire Roman Abramovich bought Chelsea Football Club for £150 million on 1 July 2003. Six days later CF Barcelona announced that they were £115 million in debt.

Following the death of Queen Victoria, no football matches were played between 22 January and 9 February 1901.

In December 2000, Manchester United were officially recognised, for the third year running, as the world's richest football club with a turnover of £110.9 million. Bayern Munich, with a turnover of £83.5 million, were declared the second richest.

The number 10 shirt worn by Brazilian superstar Pelé in the 1970 World Cup finals was sold at Christie's auction room in London on 27 March 2002 for £157,750.

Bobby Moore's spare number six shirt for the 1966 World Cup final was sold at a Wolverhampton auction for £44,000 in September 1999 while Paul Gascoigne's Euro '96 number eight shirt sold for £6,400 at an auction two months later.

Elliptical goalposts were first used in 1921.

In June 2005, twelve Republic of Ireland supporters donned Hawaiian shirts and shorts thinking they were going to Faro in Portugal for a World Cup qualifying game – in fact, it was a trip to the Faroe Islands where it was foggy and damp.

In Istanbul on 25 May 2005, Liverpool became the first team to retrieve a three-goal deficit in the final of the Champions League/European Cup. They went on to beat AC Milan 3-2 on penalties after the game finished 3-3 after extra time.

Eleven different venues in London have staged full international matches.

Wigan Athletic made thirty-four unsuccessful applications to gain entry into the Football League. They finally made it with twenty-nine votes in 1978 and are now playing Premiership football.

Unable to settle at any one club, tall French striker Mickael Antoine-Curier created a new record in 2003/04 when he became the first player in the history of the Football League to be associated with six different clubs in a peacetime season. He assisted Oldham Athletic, Kidderminster Harriers, Rochdale, Sheffield Wednesday, Notts County and Grimsby Town. He had earlier served with Nancy (France), Preston North End, Nottingham Forest and Brentford from 2001, making it nine clubs in three years.

In season 2004/05 John Terry gained a Premiership winners' medal with Chelsea while his brother Paul collected a medal with Yeovil Town, who claimed the Coca-Cola League 2 title.

Dean Windass of Hull City became one of the oldest players ever to score a goal at Wembley when his winner in the Championship Play-off Final against Bristol City, shot the Tigers into the Premiership. Windass was 39 at the time.

Six Ipswich Town players appeared in the film *Escape to Victory*. They were Paul Cooper, Kevin Beattie, John Wark, Laurie Sivell, Russell Osman and Kevin O'Callaghan.

In 1952, three FA Cup ties all took place in the same suburb of London; Leyton and Hereford United drew 0–0, Leyton Orient and Bristol Rovers ended 1–1 and Leystone lost 2–0 at home to Watford.

In 2007–08 Manchester City had players from 20 different countries registered as professionals (15 of them internationals). They came from Belgium, Brazil, Bulgaria, China, Croatia, Denmark, Ecuador, Faroe Islands, France, Germany, Greece, Italy, Mexico, Nigeria, Slovakia, Spain, Sweden, Switzerland, Tunisia and Zimbabwe. They also had players from England, Scotland, Ireland and Wales.

West Ham United were the first team to win at The Emirates Stadium, beating Arsenal 1–0 in a Premiership match on 7 April 2007.

In 2009, Notts County became the first club to complete 4,500 League games.

Before entering in 1977, Wigan Athletic had made 34 unsuccessful attempts at gaining a place in the Football League, while Hartlepool had to reapply for re-election a record 11 times.

Jack Martin was associated with seven different Lancashire clubs between 1923 and 1932 – Accrington Stanley, Blackpool, Burnley, Nelson, Oldham Athletic, Southport and Wigan Borough. He also played for Macclesfield.

QRP, 4–0 down to Newcastle in 1984, fought back to earn a 5–5 draw. And in 1997 Rangers trailed Port Vale 4–1 but came back to draw 4–4.